EVANESCENCE

EVANESCENCE
Selected Poems

WALLY SWIST

SHANTI ARTS PUBLISHING

BRUNSWICK, MAINE 04011

EVANESCENCE
Selected Poems

Published by Shanti Arts Publishing
Interior and cover design by Shanti Arts Designs

Shanti Arts LLC
193 Hillside Road
Brunswick, Maine 04011

shantiarts.com

Poems from *Candling the Eggs, The Map of
Eternity,* and *The Bees of the Invisible* were previously
published by Shanti Arts Publishing.

Image on cover and page 1 by
Michele Bergami / unsplash.com

Printed in the United States of America

ISBN: 978-1-951651-14-5 (softcover)
ISBN: 978-1-951651-20-6 (hardcover)

Library of Congress Control Number: 2020934930

For the Readers of These Poems
and
for Tevis Kimball

The most beautiful thing we can experience is the mysterious. It is the source of all true art and science.
—Albert Einstein

Contents

from *Veils of the Divine (1998)*

from *Luminous Dream (2010)*

from *Winding Paths Worn through Grass (2010)*

from *Huang Po and the Dimensions of Love (2012)*

from *Blessing and Homage (2012)*

from *Velocity (2013)*

from *Invocation (2015)*

from *Things I Know I Love: Odes to Food (2015)*

from *Candling the Eggs (2017)*

from *The View of the River (2017)*

from *The Map of Eternity (2017)*

from *The Bees of the Invisible* (2019)

New Poems (2020)

Acknowledgments

Grateful acknowledgment is made to the editors of the following publications where these poems were initially published, often in earlier versions.

2River Review: "Rats in the Barn"
The 3288 Review: "Anita," "Brook Run," "Meeting Amichai," "Present Time"
Adelaide Literary Journal: "*Oh, What a Pity:* An Ode to Paula Modersohn-Becker"
Alimentum: The Literature of Food: "Cinnamon Sticks," "The Lawrence Durrell *Alexandria Quartet* Mediterranean Cold Plate Dinner Special," "Ode to End of Summer"
all roads will lead you home: "Deer, in Three Movements," "The Wood"
Angel Face: "Threshold"
Appalachia (Appalachia Mountain Club): "Black-eyed Susan," Branta," "Catalpa," "Confluence," "Daylilies," "Deer Park," "Fox," "Hawk Feathers," "Heron," "Milk Snake," "Morning Snowfall, Haskins' Meadow," "Northfield Mountain Pond," "Salmon Brook," "Roaring Falls: Mid-March," "Sharp-Shinned Hawk," "Snow Geese," "Top of the Ridge," "Tracks of Deer," "The Veil," "Vixen," "A Way of Seeing," "Whitetails," "Wild Falling"
Apple Valley Review: A Journal of Contemporary Literature: "The Annunciation"
Arabesques Review (Algeria): "If It Is Meant To Be"
Arts: The Arts in Theological and Religious Studies: "The Rain in October"
The Ashvamegh International Journal & Literary Magazine (India): "The Enchanted Tailor," "Heart's Essence"

Basilica Review: "Backlit in a Wash of Light"
Blue Lyra Review: "Dinner with Camus"
Blueline: "Opossum," "Skiers"
Blood and Honey Review: "Blessing"
Buddhist Poetry Review: "Gyoto Monks," "Satori"

Caesura (Poetry Center San Jose): "Pandan"
The Cape Rock: "Experiencing the Light," "In Memory of Jack Gilbert"
carte blanche (Canada): "Autumn: Ansonia, 1962"
Chiron Review: "The Map of Eternity," "Roman Numerals"
Clockhouse Review: "The Victrola on the Label"
Connecticut Review: "Honey Locust," "Small Miracles"
Connecticut River Review: "Gathering Sweetness," "Ode to the Iris," "The Snail"

Common Ground Review: "Breaking Open Garlic"
Commonweal: "Dominic Savio," "Rilkean Dream," "September Morning"
Crab Orchard Review: "Black-eyed Susan," "Frittata," "The Treadle and the Light"
Crosswinds Poetry Journal: "The Streaming"

Dappled Things: A Quarterly of Ideas, Art, & Faith: "Green Olives," "Interstices," "Mint," "Sunnyside-up in a Blanket"
De La Mancha: Art and Poetry: "Ode to the Holyoke Range"
The Deronda Review: "Green Lake, Ellsworth, Maine," "Prayer for Yoram Raanan"

Earth First: "The City of Nails," "The Owl"
EarthSpeak: "Bloodroot Open Before Trillium"
Empirical Magazine: "Homage to Ed Ricketts," "In the Shade of a Cave"
Eureka Street (Australia): "Cameo," "Finding my Grandfather," "The Sunflowers," "The View of the River," "Walt Whitman on Donald Trump," "What We Ever Really Need to Know"

FutureCycle Poetry: "Recognition"

The Galway Review (Ireland): "The Blind," "The Female Cardinal," "Grand Wizard," "Green Herons," "Gothic," "A Holiday Menu: Respite and Cheer," "In Memory of Galway Kinnell," "Ode to my New Shoes," "Poem after James Wright's 'In Fear of Harvests,'" "Ley Lines," "Remembering Ruth Stone," "Salutations: after Antonio Porchia," "Something Worth Aspiring To," "Sooey," "Suicide Vest," "Sun Worship," "Written Upon the Death of W. S. Merwin"
The Guidebook: "Ode to February"

Halcyon (Canada): "Apples"

Kentucky Review: "An Act of Love"

Lalitamba: "The Locomotive"
The Larcom Review: "Guardian Angel," "Starflower"
Litbreak: "The Day after the 2016 Election," "New Paint on Worn Walls," "The Space Between," "The Swist"
The Literary Bohemian: "My Friends, the Bees"
Longhouse: "The Dog of Poetry"
Lungfish Review: "Dogwood"

Many Hands: A Magazine for Holistic Health: "The Autumnal,"
  "Destinations," "Cinnamon and Honey," "Huang Po and the Dimensions
  of Love," "The Locomotive," "Mount Toby, Spring Thaw," "Mystery,"
  "Visiting Jack Gilbert at Fort Juniper," "The New Life," "Ode to Open
  Meadow," "Silhouette," "Snowy Owl," "Tone Poem for Summer Solstice,"
  "Walking Stick"
Mudfish: "Left Unsaid"

New England Watershed Magazine: "Living in the Moment"
North American Review: "The Knowing"
Numinous: Spiritual Poetry: "The Pendulum"

Old Crow: "Before Dawn"
Osiris: "Coyotes," "Ennui," "Life Pulse," "My Death," "Roaring Brook,"
  "Shamisen," "Shells," "The Skunk," "Swallow," "Starflower," "Taking It
  Back with Me," "The Use of Natural Objects"
Out of Many: A Multi-cultural Literary Magazine: "Eulogy," "Thirteen
  Ways of Remembering Lonnie Black"
Outerbridge: "After Putting my Dog Down," "Helping Hands," "The Red
  Fox," "Whiskey"

Painted Bride Quarterly: "Sweet Woodruff"
Peacock Journal: "Evanescence," "The Practiced Silence"
Perfume River Poetry Journal: "Summer Rain"
Poet Lore: "Twilight"
Poetry Salzburg (Austria): "The Dante Alighieri *Paradiso Summer Al
  Fresco*"
Puckerbrush Review: "The Gingko," "Great Blue," "Listening To Rilke,"
  "Moving the Woodpile," "October," "Ode to the Omelette," "Ode to
  Squash Soup," "Practicing Mindfulness," "Putting Up the Mailbox"
Pulchritude: "The Jay, the Rope, and the Snake"
Pulp Literature (Canada): "What Is Essential"

Rattle: "Nautilus Shell," "The Ringing of Silence"
The RavensPerch: Adding Breath to Words: "Purple Iris," "Presence on
  the Mountain," "Ravening," "Tzu-jan," "Wandering Mazily," "Woodland
  Frogs"
Red Fox Review: "I Look Out on a Dark Road: A Poem for my Father"
River Poets Journal: "After Having Stacked the Cord the Day Before," "The
  Language of Our Hands"
riverrun magazine (Quincy University): "The Word"

Sahara: A Journal of New England Poetry: "Blue," "Cushman Brook, Early October," "Kisses," "Neruda," "Fort Juniper, Midsummer," "March Wind," "Radiance," "Snowdrops, Fort Juniper," "Trailing Arbutus"

Sanctuary: The Massachusetts Audubon Magazine: "The Rush of the Brook Stills the Mind"
Scree: "Negatives"
Slant: A Journal of Poetry: "Dry Ledges"
Snowy Egret: "Desire," "The Geese," "Walking the Meadow in Autumn"
SPANK the CARP: "Reawakening"
Still Point Arts Quarterly: "The Chakras as Flower Essences," "Ode to Jack LaLanne," "Spring Rain"
Sufi: Journal of Mystical Philosophy & Practice: "The Bees of the Invisible"

Telephone: "Amputee's Litany"
Theodate: "Blue Chicory"
Third Wednesday: "Augury," "The Hallway," "The Leper," "Ode to Presence"
Tuck: A Magazine for Discerning Readers (Canada): "Abhorrence," "Distance," "Imminence," "Lloyd," "Porcupine," "To Discernment," "Trump"
The Tule Review: "Flowering"

upstreet: "The Mice of Fort Juniper"

The Wayfarer: A Journal of Contemplative Literature: "Bouquet"
The Whirlwind Review: "Long Mountain," "Quintessence"
Wild River Review: "A Field of Sunflowers"
The Woven Tale Press: "Cinema," Hydrangea," "Rilke, at Chateau de Muzot"

The Yale Literary Magazine: "Quiet," "The Voice"
Yankee Magazine: "Cider," "Hurricane"

Zymbol: The Magazine of Symbolism & Surrealism: "Dream Time"

"After Reading *The Upanishads*" was anthologized in an earlier version in *Between the Lines: A Gathering of Writings by Booksellers* (Barnes & Noble Books, 1996).
"Aftermath" originally appeared in an earlier version in *The Duchess of Malfi's Apricots and Other Literary Fruit* (Columbia, South Carolina: University of South Carolina Press).

"Autumn: Ansonia, 1962" was reprinted in *Poetry Salzburg Review* (Austria).

"Black-eyed Susan" was published in an earlier version in *Crab Orchard Review.*

"Blue Chicory" was reprinted in a revised version in the print journal *Blueline.*

"Breaking Open Garlic" was reprinted in *Arabesques Review* (Algeria).

"The Chakras, as Flower Essences" appeared online in *all roads will lead you home.*

"The City of Nails" was anthologized in *What Poets See* (FutureCycle Press, 2012).

"For Walt Whitman" was published as a limited edition letterpress broadside by master printer Clarence Wolfshohl at his El Grito del Lobo Press. The poem was also anthologized in *Bliss* (Muse Press).

An earlier version of "Fox," entitled "Reynard," was published in *Crosswinds Poetry Journal.*

"The Geese" was anthologized in *What's Nature Got to Do With Me: Staying Wildly Sane in a Mad World* (Native West Press, 2012).

"Guardian Angel" was anthologized in *Sunken Garden Poetry: 1992-2011* (Wesleyan University Press, 2012).

"Heirloom" was distinguished as a finalist in the 2015 Littoral Press broadside contest and was published as a letterpress limited edition broadside by fine printer Lisa Rappoport.

"Heron" and "The Red Fox" were anthologized in the online edition of *Sunken Garden Poetry: 1992-2011* (Wesleyan University Press, 2012).

"Heron" and "Swallows" were set to music for piano and soprano by Dr. Douglas Bruce Johnson, an Emeritus Associate Professor of Music of Trinity College, Hartford, Connecticut.

"Hurricane" was anthologized in the *1995/1996 Anthology of Magazine Verse and Yearbook of American Poetry* (Monitor Book Company, Inc., 1997).

An earlier version of "Interstices" was published in *Blueline.*

"In the Shade of a Cave" was anthologized in *Weatherings* published by FutureCycle Press in their Good Works Series.

"March Wind" was collected in *Solace in So Many Words* (Hourglass Books/Weighed Words, 2011).

An earlier version of "The Mice of Fort Juniper" was a finalist in the 2015 Mudfish Poetry Contest, and was published in the magazine.

"Mystery" was reprinted in *Arabesques Review* (Algeria).

"Ode to Jack LaLanne" appeared online in an earlier version in *Tuck: A Magazine for Discerning Readers* (Canada).

The first four lines of "Ode to Open Meadow" appeared in *The Artist and the American Landscape* (First Glance Books, 1998).

"Outside the Box" was anthologized in *American Society: What Poets See* (FutureCycle Press).

"Putting Up the Mailbox" was issued as a limited edition letterpress broadside by Timberline Press.

"The Rain in October" was nominated for a Pushcart Prize.

"Satori" was anthologized in *Bliss* published by Muse Press.

"Shells" was anthologized in *Stories from Where We Live: The North Atlantic Coast* (Milkweed Editions, 2000).

"The Rush of the Brook Stills the Mind" was composed to electroacoustical music written by Professor Elainie Lillios, of Bowling Green University, and performed by percussionist Scott Deal, in Jordan Hall at the New England Conservatory of Music, in June 2014.

"A Wild Beauty" was anthologized in *Except for Love: New England Poets Inspired by Donald Hall*, Edited by Cynthia Brackett-Vincent (Farmington, ME: Encircle Publications: 2019)

"Wild Falling" was selected to be printed on a granite column in Edmands Park in Newton, Massachusetts, as part of the city's Poetry in the Park Project.

These poems were published in the following collections, several now out of print: *Waking Up the Ducks* (Adastra Press, 1987), *For the Dance* (Adastra Press, 1991), *The New Life* (Plinth Books, 1998), *Veils of the Divine* (Hanover Press, 2003), *Luminous Dream* (FutureCycle Press, 2010), *Winding Paths Worn through Grass* (Virtual Artists Collective, 2012), *Huang Po and the Dimensions of Love* (Southern Illinois University Press, 2012), *Velocity* (Virtual Artists Collective, 2013), *Invocation* (Lamar University Literary Press, 2015), *Things I Know I Love: Odes to Food* (Finishing Line Press, 2015), *The View of the River* (Kelsay Books/White Violet Press, 2017), *Candling the Eggs* (Shanti Arts, LLC, 2017), *The Map of Eternity* (Shanti Arts, LLC, 2018), and *A Bird Who Seems to Know Me: Poems and Haiku Regarding Birds and Nature* (Ex Ophidia Press, 2019).

Some of the following poems appeared in *Mount Toby Poems*, a letterpress limited edition, published by Timberline Press of Fulton, Missouri, with thanks to master printer Clarence Wolfshohl. Also, some of these poems were collected in *Blessing and Homage*, a letterpress limited edition published by Timberline Press, of Charlestown, Massachusetts, with appreciation to fine printer Regina Schroeder.

Acknowledgment is made to the Connecticut Commission on the Arts for an Artists Fellowship in Poetry in 2003 that facilitated the writing of the initial drafts of some of the poems that were to become *Huang Po and the Dimensions of Love.*

Grateful appreciation is made to the Robert Francis Trust for awarding me two back-to-back one-year residencies at Fort Juniper, the Robert Francis Homestead, in Cushman, Massachusetts, during 2003-2005, where the early drafts of some of these poems were composed and on a rare occasion, where the poems themselves were finished.

The author wishes to offer his appreciation to the following philanthropic literary agencies for granting financial assistance while some of these poems were written and finished: The Authors League Fund, of New York City, which provided several grants of financial aid; The Carnegie Fund for Authors, of New York City; The Haven Foundation, of Brewer, Maine; PEN America, of New York City; and Poets in Need, of Berkeley, California, which awarded the author with the assistance of a Philip Whalen Memorial Grant.

from

Waking up the Ducks

(1987)

The Dog of Poetry

After the introspective reprimands;
after the Russian roulette of the job market;

after the hoopla of executives;
after the irate customer

complains about you to superiors;
after reruns of *Magnum* and *Simon and Simon*;

after neo-conservative politicians reiterate
Ronald Reagan's words, in his saying *cockamamie*,

to comparable wages for women;
after seeing an ad for another sequel of *Rambo*;

after the cripple burned himself in the shower
due to neglect;

after the loud drunken neighbor on a hot night;
after authorities find *notes to loved ones*

at the site of the plane crash;
after untangling the fishing line

as quietly as a breakdown;
after the corporate brainwashing;

after buckling up for the long distance commute;
after news of death squads,

suicide bombings, and the acquitted rapist;
after listening to the oppressed

broadcast via Star-Wars satellite —
I feed the hungry dog of poetry.

The City of Nails

Here it is, up ahead, beyond
     that hairpin turn where
          old values are blacklisted,

where law abides by its own
     private pool of sewage
          curiously like poor Narcissus,

where death is the street punk
     telling us this is the arrival,
          the departure no one has ever

prepared for enough,
     where inverted road signs
          map the new archetype

and billboards advertise
     wash-and-wear sex,
          the most refreshing colas,

totems of refined taste, where
     the marriage of anima and animus
          is just another one-night stand

for machisma and machismo.
     Here it is. Go ahead.
          Welcome to the city of nails

where every telephone pole
     lining the farthest limits
          to the main strip is condemned

for crucifixion. Bear down.
     Head on the dark side
          unravels like black crepe.

Veleda

Small dog guests thought large,
adoring Weimaraner who ran to me

when I returned from work,
whom the vet called a *bad dog*,

that nothing could be done with
but put to sleep, friend to me

when the world ground me down
into its bitter syrup that festers

without panacea on sleepless nights,
I yielded to my own canine ways.

Amputee, Miami, 1959

He clutches brown-bag Thunderbird
beneath the shade of the Woolworth's

awning, spread like a pelican's wing.
His casters grease the pavement with a slick

roar that stops us as cold as a ball bearing.
Women scrape heels where his knuckles grind,

as they walk by, self-righteous and suburban
in tight sweaters. Our shock eye to eye

is the glazed stare of dead fish, our barracuda
nightmares, Key West shark attacks.

His cart's path in the dust is a trail
of loose ribbons, palm fronds, his holy spirit.

Hibiscus, I hear him say, *I just want*
to dip my legs in clear water.

Twilight

The sun beaches up
amid the sky's dark islands.

Night slips
over palms of clouds floating

downward among
the sinking deck of mountains.

Sophie

shuffles in the hall in her slippers.
She speaks to herself in Polish

and in English. She asks you the time,
and what is for breakfast, for lunch,

and for dinner. She asks you
how you are, and rarely steps outside.

Years of psychiatric drugs
have made her tongue stick out.

Even after her single mastectomy,
she still keeps her money

tied in a roll around her neck
in the cleavage beneath her housecoat.

She makes sense of the world.
Sometimes she even sings.

from

For the Dance

(1991)

Coyotes

Two a.m., howling begins
on the edge of one of the farms left

in this valley, near the wetland
a developer has mown.

Such pure sound pierces the night,
this bloodletting beneath Orion,

this ghostly choir of thin cries
that tremble like Shawmut and Massasoit

come back to haunt us.
Then the baying of one hound

sets another hound baying
from the far rim of the opposite ridge.

Porch lights flicker
on the water of this delirious music,

and the wild pack in each of us
rises into song.

Shells

As she taught the alphabet my mother collected shells,
mounting polished conchs, augers, sundials, and whelk

in a glass case on velvet. As a child, I recited
the alphabet as waves rolled from the sea to land.

I have never lost the words found in a harbor, the shells
brought home from the beach. I still pocket them

as I walk the shore and press some
to my ear so that I can listen again to the beginning.

Life Pulse

a sequence written for some of the compositions
performed by the Japanese percussion
ensemble Kodo, on their One Earth Tour

Hae

the eaves drip
with winter rain —
the timpani
of steel drum
becomes water.

Ryogen No Hi

a flame spreads
wide across the fields;
the clash of hand cymbals
leads a herd of wild horses
through the smoke.

Kari Uta

the sweet high tone
of bamboo flute
calls us home —
the forgotten taste
of wine.

Chonlima

keeping pace with
the One Thousand League Horse
that races into the distance —
drumsticks in a storm
of percussion.

Yatai Bayashi
> the life pulse beats
> as we strain
> to pull our carts —
> again. it is time
> for the festival.

Yu Karak
> after a day in the fields,
> the farmer rejoices —
> a hoe on his shoulder.
> oats, rice, barley . . .
> here, come take my hand.

Whiskey

Near the hedges he watched his father kill black snakes —
the hoe's edge sliced thick writhing coils.

He swallowed a fly, and his mother went into the kitchen,
returning with whiskey; *It will kill the germs,*

do not tell your father. Things grew heavy —
the twilight deepened in sepia tones, the swing set

assembled by his father glowed in amber,
and he shuffled to bed through the buzz of television

in neighboring houses. When the story was told,
he expected ire, the red hot flare of his father's temper,

those strong hands pounding the countertop,
but, instead, all three recoiled in unison, laughing.

Negatives

A friend returns negatives of photographs
you took of each other years ago.

You sent the originals
back home to other friends to show them

how well you were doing.
Now you hold negatives up to the light,

and count what is lost a frame at a time.
You hold them high as if you were being robbed.

My Friends, the Bees

for John Maziarz

The winter night you helped me
untie the mattress from the top of the car,

and we carried it upstairs, all you said was:
We will find a river. With that I was alerted

to the currents that flowed inside you.
Then into spring and through fall, you held

ladders, while I painted tall Victorian peaks
and gripped the shutters you handed to me;

more than just the stickiness of paint between us.
You began stories with *Well, yass,*

and I followed you coon hunting over expanses
of swamp abundant with pussy willow.

You would punch the time clock the next morning
at the factory, spent, but full of the river

you had found. That next spring at dusk,
when the smell of damp earth rises, you led me

to the abandoned servants' quarters, only days
before a doctor's diagnosis of cancer, and there,

where a broken water pipe made a right angle
over the blossoming hawthorn, came the dripping

from the hive, that first covered your index finger,
then flowed over your entire hand with a buzzing

that matched the quiver in your voice,
when you declared, *My friends, the bees.*

Recognition

A man dreams about the child
deep within him, and a train of many cars

passes through the dream with a familiar
face behind each window.

In the passing of cars, he sees
his own face as it appears in the dream,

and the light within him shines
in each window and reflects his childhood.

In the reflection of his face, the child
deep within him awakens from a dream.

Morning Snow, Haskins' Meadow

Blown clouds bury the day moon,
snow turns the wind white, fills fox tracks

across the meadow to the brook. A towhee
calls beyond the frozen ledge of burdock

ahead on the path through the hawthorn.
I clamber over alders fallen

across a gully of ground pine — pheasant wings'
sudden drum from a hemlock grove —

the green head, the eyes' red ornament, the golden
plumage through a spray of snow ascending.

Tracks of Deer

The last dusk gathers the troughs
and deep wells into its darkness;

the moon assumes its place beside
the silo's reflection; a cloud of midges

condenses the air above the pond.
Winding paths worn through grass

cross the meadow suffused with lunar light.
I bend down, touch the earth.

Small Miracles

Barn swallows, those dark handkerchiefs,
that drop from the sky and lift

again, find a place to perch,
then pause on a rim of a perfect arc.

I also fly into the eternity of an image
like the cricket,

that black jewel,
who sings about nothing but this all night.

The Owl

I am awakened by cries that do not stop.
They say, Come, see if you can find me—

half the meadow in moonlight,
the other half shadowed by white pine.

A pair of eyes fly up and dance:
owl eyes that hold the moon.

from

The New Life

(1998)

Dogwood

Whose flowers
      seem to float
            along its limbs,
                  as a mobile

placed in the air,
      as delicate as the word
            for slenderness,
                  hosomi, in Japanese.

Whose petals
      bear the imprint
            of the red-rimmed
                  kiss of the princess

of blossoming trees.
      Whose suchness
            evokes the exclamation,
                  Ah.

Whose blown blossoms
      become a small rain,
            conjuring Lao Tzu,
                  who lectured

beneath it about
      Tao, and suggested
            the middle path
                  can be found

in the calligraphy
      of dogwood petals
            as they write themselves
                  on a page of the wind.

The New Life

Every morning, the rooster
    awakens me to begin my day.
        He projects the scratchy

tenor of his voice,
    on whose squeaking hinges
        doors open to the new life.

Given the chance,
    as he has, he would like
        to awaken the world,

and as sunlight streams
    through the leaves
        down the mountain, I rise

from my bed in a cabin
    at the bottom of a hill, and
        go to work; my dreams

still moist with dew
    from the night before.
        Rooster, you call the morning

light that illumines
    a new beginning, and even
        in gray weather, with the rain

of sleet thundering over
    the shed's corrugated tin roof,
        it is your voice, friend,

that rings out
    to affirm the possibility
        of weathering any storm.

Ode to Open Meadow

This is where wildflowers and winds
blossom and end —

verdure bordered by stone walls,
whose track, worn by farm wagons

piled high with bales of hay,
rises and disappears in morning fog.

Scent of cedar and scrub juniper,
glimmer of stone outcrops —

sulphurs wind a trail between a patch
of purple clover and shoals of anemones,

then alight upon each marsh buttercup
dotting the bluestems.

I am cleansed in watching the quiet ways
of the foraging spotted doe,

how swallows pluck gnats from a cloud
that expands and contracts

beneath Venus and the crescent,
as if I had died and entered the *bardo*,

that time of blessing
for the soul in between lives.

Desire

All summer, vines and bramble
block the path to the brook.
Black snakes slide through the weeds.

I can see the light shine on the field
of corn stubble that stretches across
the flats. I beat back briers and tangles

of nettles beneath the grove of sumac
choked with a new growth of alders.
A startled pheasant flies up.

Feathers float in a cloud of dust,
coyote and raccoon tracks printed
deep in the mud. Each year

more trees have fallen. I toss
what I can out of the way; sometimes
a rotted trunk breaks in my arms.

The brook runs high and fast
from autumn rains and pounds over
the stones. If I stop to listen,

I hear the wind snap a branch
of white pine, deer browse in the grass.
I find myself going further, further.

Destinations

We're in such a hurry
  that we miss
    our true destinations —
      we need to observe

that flock of pigeons
  along the way,
    roosting on
      a flat roof

pebbled with
  white stones,
    cooing and contented
      in the late warmth

of November
  sun, beyond which
    lies the river,
      and its reflection,

throbbing
  as it flows,
    before it empties
      into the sea.

We need to remember
  to return
    to the source,
      whose center

can be referenced
  anywhere, blessed
    by the name
      beyond names;

transcribed by us,
    through each act,
        our auras pulsing,
            as in knowing

when one has
    finally arrived,
        crouched among
            the stones,

hiking
    snowy mountain,
        the stream
            having drawn us

off the trail,
    as if the light
        were a sound
            rushing in our ears.

The Red Fox

I am sure of the tracks
    this morning in new snow
        that veer off the meadow path

past the conical stumps
    bordering the edge of young willows
        and angle towards the beaver lodge

beyond the dogleg of the brook
    from which a cloud of steam drifts
        downstream heading south.

Doubling back out of the grove,
    I lose sense of its direction, but
        as I look up, I see the fox there

in the meadow, high-stepping
    in the snow, moving with stealth
        to study the ground as it follows

mouse tracks between snow tunnels.
    It does not see me until it stops
        just ten yards away, and I cease

breathing as it lifts its head, eyes wide
    and as bright as black agates, the hue
        of its coat ecstatic in the sunlight,

and for an instant we are locked
    in stillness before it streaks past
        birch and poplar and into a thicket

of white pine to disappear so quickly
    it leaves a tint that lingers like breath
        on the cold morning air.

Catalpa

This is what succulence is: the trumpets of your blossoms
spilled across the path, the centers of their white funnels

striped orange and spotted purple. Inhaling their fragrance,
I am unaware of the source until I find myself

standing beneath you. As a trail of fallen petals
disappears into the swale, your broad heart shaped leaves

rocking from the branches of your massive crown
send a shudder through me in the sudden coolness of this rain.

Hurricane

The shutters applaud themselves
with lunatic frenzy. The hinges
have swallowed their tongues.

A weatherman's voice fizzles
in a gasp of static. The wind
lifts fists of stone.

Shingles are stripped, windows
go blind, and all the echoes
clench their teeth.

As you light the candles,
lightning brushing our shadows,
splinters like glass.

Walking the Meadow in Autumn

Withered flowers of goldenrod
rock in the wind, silver with frost.

A thistle seed, freed from thorns,
sails the air. A marsh hawk

circles, riding an updraft.
Grass, trampled beneath

the barbed wire fence, stirs,
where, more than once,

I have seen a dark shape slip away
at dusk. A porcupine plods

through the brush, emerges,
retreats, quills raised and quivering.

Quickly, in the sunlight, a vixen
disappears into a grove of spruce.

As unlucky as my life has been,
stuck on the Great Wheel of Being,

I count myself fortunate to hear,
far off, a bell that jars the heart.

Starflower

Star of the upland woodlands,
seven-petaled, not unlike

the Pleiades' seven sisters,
you speckle the new green

of the undergrowth beside
the loose talus of the trail

like flecks of sea foam amid
a bed of browned pine needles.

Wherever you bloom, starflower,
your china white blazes, fixed

like a pattern of starlight,
your petals a constellation

set among the shade spread along
the mountain path every May.

I see you everywhere
since now I know your name.

Whitetails

Turning my head
  at the crack
    of a fallen branch,

Whitetails, I say,
  spotting two does.
    They bound away

into the sedge,
  and zigzag
    over the hummocks,

the undersides
  of their tail patches
    silky-tufted

like open milkweed pods.
  In mid-leap, suspended,
    they vanish

into the fallen dusk
  already glittering
    with early frost.

After Putting My Dog Down

Her blonde Labrador's fur blends
with the shaft of sunlight I let in
after finally opening that door to

the room at the vet's. I leave her
as if she were waiting for me any
Saturday morning — head on paws,

tail curled in a wagging abeyance,
patient, as she always was,
so help me, I thought I could learn

that virtue from her, always ready
for my call to come: *Come Cider,
let's go for a walk to the brook.*

Sweet Woodruff

for Robert Francis

Those slips of sweet woodruff
you gave as gift stand in tribute
to our visits. We brought fruit,

looked up words you had saved
so they could be as crystalline as
our friendship, and grounded in trust,

like those slips of sweet woodruff
that have taken root with an aroma
that permeates our memory.

from

Veils of the Divine

(1998)

Scrub Meadow

At the foot of Mount Toby, on a rise above Cranberry Pond,
I wade through clusters of St. John's-wort's yellow corollas.

A dragonfly bends back a bristly stem of bottlebrush grass.
The rayed flowers of yarrow offer a sweet aroma

when rubbed between fingers into the palm.
I brush tall blooms of mullein that open out a softness

from their basal leaves. Candles of their petals burn bright
in the hot July sun. I watch grasshoppers vault

pearly stands of sweet white clover. I find the meadow within,
waist-deep in fleabane, turning the wind lavender.

Heron

Any movement now will release it
from its stance; stick legs that wade

across the silt of the bog,
wings folded like slate blue sails

that may unfurl, the smooth, quick
rocking of its body

that stabs the water with its long bill,
the wriggling fish that descends

the curve of its gullet.
Peering, it listens, neck now straight,

we, too, bent forward, alert, sinking
into the mud, into the stillness that spreads

among us, the dull glimmer of ripples
rimmed with dusk across the wetland.

Opening its wings, the heron glides unseen,
touches down again among the reeds.

Northfield Mountain Pond

This morning taking Rose Ledge Trail up
Northfield Mountain through the peak

color of autumn woods, I am
aware of having lived other lives.

A turkey vulture spirals above me.
I run my hand over a black birch trunk,

the nubbed scars of bear claw
marks along its smooth bark.

Before leaving, I watch
through mist a great blue heron

fishing the pond, its presence deepening
the post-dawn peace, the inimitable

silence, broken only by the
plash from a dripping beak.

Salmon Brook

Chute after chute of white
water spreads over boulders.

The sluice curls ledge to ledge,
slides from bend to bend.

A cascade surges towards a confluence.
Upstream a hawk's shadow ripples.

I have awakened to a life
I dreamed of living — spray

prismed in light, torrent
casting farther into mist, into cloud.

Ode to the Omelette

I dice onions
      that remind me of Renoir's
            painting of onions,

of onions so real I weep.
      I crush cloves of garlic,
            that are all pungence,

a shaman's breath,
      the kitchen's verb.
            I chop green flags

of scallions, and ripened
      from my garden, slice a tomato,
            that becomes a song

when cut into wedges,
      dripping with seeds, as fragrant
            as the garden itself.

All of this goes into
      the hot olive oil, now sizzling
            now blessing the air.

I beat eggs, pour them into
      the skillet, and because I am
            happy, spread a handful

of grated cheddar over the top.
      I finish this with paprika for color,
            cayenne for spicy heat,

tarragon for its gracious
     offering of sweetness.
          Carefully I fold it,

and now it is done; sliding
     from the spatula onto the plate,
          my ode to the morning.

Swallows

I ask the swallows that perch on the wire
between the shed and the barn:

*Where have you flown? And just
how many ponds did you dip into?*

They chatter back at me, then lose
patience, and return to their loop after loop

through the shed's missing windows.
I will sit awhile longer in the dusk,

until the swallows become shadows,
and the stars, that begin to flicker, shower

the blue bowl of this valley, and imagine
myself flying through the spaces.

Guardian Angel

after Rolf Jacobsen

For years I have been trying to find the patience
to listen to the resonant whisper of her voice
tickling my ear. Sometimes I imagine I see her,

the one who keeps me calm, whose guiding hands
steer me out of the shallows of my own making;
who walks on a cool, dustless path; who presses

her head against my heart, whose arms around
my shoulders lift by morning; who awakens in me
a vision of the ruby in the hummingbird's song.

Cider

Yellow Labrador, companion, happy tail that greeted me,
who was named after the color of her fur, the sweetness

of her disposition, who jumped out of a half open
car window to follow me across the highway, and a semi's

brakes locked to avoid her. Trapped on an outcrop
ten feet above me that first summer, hiking Mount Toby's

rock ledges, she believed in me
enough to leap when I called and I caught her in my arms.

Ennui

after Giuseppe Ungaretti

I pick things up, put them down,
walk from room to room.

The moths of my best intentions
flood the streetlights.

The Rush of the Brook Stills the Mind

The trail flashes
>with sluices of snowmelt.
>>Silver-green undersides

of hemlock lift in the wind.
>A warbler's electric call
>>climbs all the way

up the mountain slope.
>That hidden waterfall
>>we promised to see

this spring unrolls bolt after bolt
>of runoff that splashes
>>veils of watery lace

over stones. The canopy
>creaks with pine siskins.
>>Mist rises above snow.

The aloneness almost too much
>for one man. The surge
>>of the brook crashes

around boulders; a sinkhole
>swirls and dips. Ripples
>>cascade in a basin

under deadfall to plunge
>into a froth of torrent.
>>A nuthatch debugs

a fallen branch that rocks
>in the current; and a mayfly
>>is blown above the spray.

Helping Hands

Some days are worth it: you forgive
a friend's indiscretions, the boss smiles,

you catch the crystal vase before
it hits the floor, that pain in your chest

is inexplicably gone.
People's faces brighten when they see

your dog leaning out the back seat
window, her ears flapping in the wind.

You listen to your inner voice —
it urges you to drive the long way home.

A goldfinch's song rings from a nearby tree.
You allow your imagination

to take you places. Those invisible hands
helping you all day suddenly become wings.

from

Luminous Dream

(2010)

Active Grace

We speak of the challenge of being able to articulate bliss.
She brings about rapture in me whenever we are together.

It is my experience that it is not just energy,
that it is not pedestrian, that it perpetuates itself between us.

I find this consistent and beyond any expectations.
We both seek *Atman* and *Brahman* in ourselves, although

I find sustenance, without dogma, a touchstone within her.
Something as rhapsodic as this can be heard

in the music of Brahms's *Variations on a Theme by Haydn.*
In the rigors of something that beautiful resounding

across the keyboards of two pianos on the CD player,
I go back to it, then not getting enough, go back again.

Aftermath

We talk cautiously of differences: how the fragrance of roses
opens in the heat of the afternoon, how honey locust blossoms

are most fragrant in evening coolness, how the shape
of the beech leaf opposes the chestnut, the first saw-toothed,

the latter elliptical, notched, the tips tapered.
We remark how ferns have uncurled their green fists into fronds.

We walk back into the meadow, find patches of strawberries
we pluck by the handful. You dispose one after another

into my mouth. The tart sweetness sears my tongue.
Beneath the bluest possible sky, the whole field burns with blossoms.

Luminous Dream

I can still feel the pull of her body toward mine
in the dream, afterward like the tide,

and hear her say: *No man has ever waited for me*
the way you have. You have waited like no other.

When we begin to work on cleaning
an Oriental rug, and we brush away layers of thick dust,

the design of the blue, green, and red feathers
of a Painted Bunting are revealed in the pattern

woven into the pile. The entire dream
unfolds in a lustrous light that is not only magnified

exponentially but also released as the bird is freed.
That occurs both in the dream and upon waking

on this plane. She will always be an incandescence
burning within me. What a journey the light has taken us on.

Neruda

It is not impossible, or mutually exclusive,
for one person to love another:

one who is familiar with opulence
and one who understands what opulence is.

Once, you told me, Neruda
wrote about love as being unloosened

like seawater. Now when I think of you,
it is wave after wave of ocean I hear.

The Ringing of Silence

They are not in any hurry, there are fewer expectations.
What is different this time is their stillness,

but not what is delicious about their familiarity.
They learn through the practice of separation

how to become more tender.
After she takes off her dress, she asks him

for one of his shirts, and he decides on the green corduroy.
She chooses to wear it unbuttoned all night.

Walking Stick

Take all away from me, but leave me Ecstasy.
Emily Dickinson

If you make a gift
of your walking stick —
make it a thick pine branch,

stripped of the bark—
the one that has accompanied you
on many hikes. Let it be the one

that has secured
your steps on Toby, Grace,
and Lafayette. Brush the wood

with layers of polyurethane,
cincture the top with a sash
of wound leather strips, tied in

a bow knot;
then insert hawk feathers
to billow above the woven cords.

En prana it
to guide her on a trail
in the wild. By your making it

a gift, *bless her*
as she walks
wherever she walks, so that she may

remember: *she is*
one with everything—
that she is safe whenever she walks.

It is imperfectly fashioned,
unlike your *Ecstasy,* but it is
designed to remind her of that.

from

Winding Paths Worn
through Grass

(2010)

ds

rough the great and
ire conscious in
es beyond sorrow.

...streaked with the sky
at dusk. When I speak

with the master at the hermitage,
he says, *You are welcome to stay*

as long you like. Once, before
waking, I hear his voice call

my name. It rings deep within me,
it vibrates like a bell, it spreads out

in ripples clear across
the water in the bright morning.

Dry Ledges

What is uncanny is the strength
that accompanies the autumn.

The oiled chirping of a cricket
penetrates the diminished

ratchet of cicadas; a passing
wedge of geese writes the symbol

for *flock* across the smoky
sky in brant, reminding me —

Fires still burn in my heart.
The sound of the rain, igniting

in the maple's crown, pulls me
toward the gravity of a falling

leaf; and these dry ledges
of the mountain stream, brightened

by a flurry of blowing beech leaves,
is the strength that carries me,

as it flows with the first silver
trickles of October rain.

The Skunk

She risks the glow of the bare
bulb that burns above the porch

to follow the lingering
scent of roses in the bed behind

the house. But her eyes, when
ours meet, look up through

the window with the chill
of October. They sparkle like

river stones, and shine before
leaving, to find stars scattered

across the meadow path
that frost takes in the moonlight.

Before Dawn

for Bert Meyers

Wind turns and turns again like a man
in his sleep. A mouse rummages

in the bureau, jarring the familiar
and the forgotten from drawer to drawer.

Birds canvass about existence;
the alarm clock buzzes like a dentist's drill.

The wind's a semi
that's driven all night past the poplars.

Rats in the Barn

As O'Keeffe forced herself to watch sidewinders
in the desert, she became inured to the undulating of her own viscera.

Old Earl, storyteller and itinerant handyman, had a similar challenge
every time he tried to quit drinking. My fear was no worse

as I walked to the barn every morning to gather brushes, ladders,
and cans of paint; to feel cold sweat bead as I listened to the rats

drag themselves across the warped boards that floored the hay loft;
to know the shadows had eyes. Only after the job was finished

and all the shutters were rehung just a day before first snow,
Old Earl announced he had shot one in the head, *Big as a cat*, he said.

Shamisen

On just these three
strings of shamisen,
listen to how

the dragonfly suddenly
hovers and darts
among the blue-green

reeds, darts
and hovers on only
these three strings.

The Voice

I am walking
in a field
of tall grass.

I hear her
call my name.
I am listening

to her voice
in the wind.
She calls me

as if she
spoke to me
from another world.

Top of the Ridge

Climbing through spring snow in Granville
State Forest, we listen for bird song.

In the wands of a sapling cherry, at the top
of the ridge, I spot a warbler's empty nest.

We stop on the talused trail — fresh snow
covers our tracks from two weeks ago.

At cliff's edge, crystals of wind-scattered
rime blown through clusters of browned

sweet fern, patches of pinweed,
the pale rose of matchstick moss.

I Look Out on a Dark Road:
A Poem for My Father

1   The trees beat wet leaves together
in the wind, and the roads
and sidewalks are slippery.
You have gone out for the night,
and I am left alone to play.
It grows late and I can't
sleep, so I wait up for you
on the porch, watching for
your car. A dozen cars pass by,
and still you haven't returned home.
A dozen more cars and the next
dozen cars go by without you.
Finally, you arrive after
I grow tired of counting cars.

2   I throw my arms around you,
your coat fragrant with rain.
I am afraid you wouldn't
come home, afraid of the dark.
Often you tell me
there is a dark road ahead
of me, dark like the folds
in your raincoat, your voice stern
and cold. Globes of rain
dripping on the porch from
your wet coat. You hug me
and make me feel warm.

3   I have grown older, less
afraid of the dark. You are
many miles away now;
in a hospital where uniformed
people shuttle you around,

wheel you up and down, feed you,
shave you, and cut your hair.
I imagine it is warm there,
and maybe you are asleep,
or listening to the rain mouthing
to the pools on the roof
and overflowing the gutters,
while the headlights of a car
reflect on your wall in the dark,
and the trees beat wet leaves
together in the wind, and the roads
and sidewalks are slippery.

from

Huang Po and the
Dimensions of Love

(2012)

October

after Antonio Machado

You will want to write the word
in broad strokes on a wall,

and the voice said: *October*,
as I waved away the golden bees all summer.

Wait, the voice said, when I swept out the cabin,
and every time I scythed the land

I cleared last autumn, *October*, the voice said.
Once, I watched mating red-tailed hawks

streak and circle around the massive trunks
of the white pines, then perch on the limbs

of two saplings, *October*,
the voice said, the limbs bent down

with their weight in the heat.
When they turned their heads,

the golden pupils of their eyes widened,
and they flew up in tandem

to cut between the thick trees on the other side
of Market Hill Road, leaving

the *key-key-key-key* of their calls
whistling in me all summer.

So, when I raked the fallen leaves and pine needles,
and finally repaired the shed door

where a red squirrel gnawed through last winter,
with some scrap pine from Cowles Lumber,

I heard the voice, *October*, and thought:
What have the golden bees of summer

been doing making honey out of my old failures?
Tonight, when I stand outside,

an owl hoots and hoots; my breath steams the air,
and the first hard frost spreads its silver crystals

through the boreal forest, then begins
to shine through the moonlight in October.

Mystery

Somehow I could tell you entered
the cabin, and before I unlock the door,

I check for the extra key beneath
the brick at the southwest corner.

Somehow I know it has been moved —
that it is not where it was before.

I imagine I can inhale the aroma
of your skin within the sweet scent

of the pine this cabin was built with.
I know how your aura moves across

any room, trailing those blue and gold lights —
how you must have listened to the wind

singing through the remaining leaves
of the trees in the late October rain.

I know what appears to be madness
sometimes can be love, that it is

something more inconsistent,
and then even more constant, and always

more beautiful than any of that —
so that it remains a mystery

that no one else, especially
the two of us, can understand.

Snow Geese

Their honking and trumpeting precede them
through the canopy of leafless trees and pine branches.

We look up to see white feathers — Oh
roundness of heavy bodies exultant in air!

We watch the wedge drive over the woods,
streaming slowly, one by one — a flurry

of black wing tips that stroke against the clouds.
Before the notes of their throats fade,

we bathe in the shower of their praise — then snow
begins to drift into the silence of their passage.

The Annunciation

after the painting by Sandro Botticelli, circa 1485

Having taken the bodily shape of a man,
Gabriel is struck by the weight
of the news he delivers upon entering

the threshold where Mary kneels,
cloistered in the room beyond;
the spoken words nearly making

the archangel stumble, his cape trailing
behind him. A gilded ray of light radiates
above his upturned wings and the sprig

of lilies he cradles in his left hand;
the transparent plane of his halo
holding a constellation of golden stars;

his right hand pulling up his gown
to brace his bowing in obeisance.
Upon hearing his greeting, Mary

is troubled, and begins to draw the folds
of her blue cloak across her breast
into converging shadow; the arc

of her halo like a divine hand placed
behind the white veil over her head.
Is this not how we respond to first hearing

any rejoicing, especially a message
that awakens in us the beginning
of understanding, of a life's path unimagined,

or if imagined, then unrealized?
How do we accept what is miraculous,
other than by looking through the portals

of the vestibule where Gabriel
is about to bend to his knees,
where the life beyond informs us

with the voice of the words we hear,
and as Mary waits for what she is to become,
we listen as the one expectant?

Visiting Jack Gilbert at Fort Juniper

He is shivering beside the hearth,
a fringed alpaca draped over his shoulders,

the shock of white hair disheveled;
his beard bearing the stubble of a few days

deep in thought of how he might outwit
Capablanca, call checkmate on his next move.

He is talking about *wabi*, the aesthetic spirit
the Japanese place in things that are worn,

or impoverished, and he recounts the beauty
and inner light of the weathered wooden

shingles of the houses in the seaside villages.
He shifts in the seat he has made of a crate

placed on end to tend the poor fire
with the iron poker, somehow the thawing

iced logs beginning to spark. He relates
how he visited a poet who played the piano,

who sang out each line to the rhythm struck
on the keys, who composed as he played

and sang as he wrote. He mentions
the man's unkempt white hair, how he just sat

at the *maestro's* feet. On the rug in front
of the hearth, I think, *Just the way I'm sitting*,

as he bends to work the poker among
the cordwood that begins to burst into flame.

Huang Po and the Dimensions of Love

Huang Po taught his students they were already
enlightened. I know of one student of Zen

who threw a translation of Huang Po
out of his apartment window, and the book,

like a block of wood, made it, on more than one
occasion, into an open trash can beside the curb.

This is not unlike the dimensions of love:
we feel the elephant ears of it, massage

the lion's paws of it, stroke the tiger's belly
of it, and are startled by the snort

steaming from the nostrils of the horse of it
that has run the field of it. We are illumined,

but we are unwilling to acknowledge its power;
so we remain unable to find what it is in ourselves

that is either *falling in love* or *agape*;
not understanding at all nor *understanding*

what is sublime. We may be able to pick through
the litter of the streets to discover a translation

of Huang Po's teaching among the trash.
We are the ones who threw it there.

We confuse seeing the wood with the true wood,
and lose each other halfway —

we see the wood of ourselves,
but miss the divine grain of the ordinary.

To Psyche

What she awakens in me is that I do recognize
her face. The light in those eyes radiant
above what is breathless. Her face changes
like the moon's phases: the crescent this morning
shining through mist, Long Mountain
deep in clouds and the dawn rising.
When we know what we want, it is just like this,
this not knowing, but thinking we know;
and all of it disappearing in the light around us.

Breaking Open Garlic

I use the base of both of my palms
to press against the bottom of the bulb.

The garlic opens into cloves that splay
across the grain of the cutting board.

When I crush the cloves so I can
peel them easily, I hear her saying,

Don't wait for me in this life, each clove
an incarnation unresolved:

some in Egypt, several in Sweden,
the last in Japan, and before her voice

dissolves like a bell, I inhale the pungent
fragrance of the unforgettable.

Sharp-Shinned Hawk

An explosion of cardinals, juncos, and black-capped
chickadees out of the nimbus

of the sugar maple's crown leaves the branches,
in one electric instant, clattering.

The sharp-shinned hawk zeros in
to settle on its target perch;

its talons curl to grip the bark.
It rides up and down: the dark flight feathers

and the under-white of its tail suggest an arrow
quivering in its mark. Still, the disappointment

of the hunt reveals itself in the unnerving, slight
twitches of tail feathers, the slow

rotation of its head from side to side.
Then it stretches out of its fierce, hunched posture,

flies up, veering out of the maple, off
on a sharp angle toward the back pasture.

Just when it begins to rise in the wind, it disappears
on the deception of exquisite bones.

Snowdrops, Fort Juniper

for Robert Francis

They bloom through each blanket
of March snow, and I am unable

to believe they are blossoming
after my winter of solitude.

When the snow melts, I can't help
but see them: these augurs of spring

that offer the fragrance
of the wind that blows over new snow,

the three white, waxy petals
on their small tubular stems

nodding among their speared leaves.
When I walk around to the west side

of the cabin, I hear Robert's voice:
Go and see the snowdrops,

always seeing more of them, and how
they spread out, not having seen them

after twenty years, but now
seeing them again for the first time.

The Locomotive

She asks me if I will remember our passion.
Seated beside a window in a Pullman,

passing through the countryside in spring,
a signpost of a village flashes before our eyes.

There is a red barn beside the station, a pond
reflecting sky, and pink blossoms falling above

the white chickens. Traveling in the locomotive
of the heart, we must always try to appraise

what we can keep and how much
of the extraordinary we must learn to let go of,

how much of us, as *limitless as passion can be,*
will remain; how we may be able

to break past that to find ourselves
more aware of a radiance than a blinding light,

destined, as we are, to arrive
somewhere between moving and standing still.

Fort Juniper, Midsummer

The sprinkling of sap pelts the understory
of hickory and maple leaves

from the towering branches of white pine.
Amber rain falls through the simmer of wind

from the canopy in the sunlight.
I sweat to the swing of each

sweep of the blade that scythes
the overgrowth around the cabin.

When I stop to rest, and lean on the handle,
curved like an egret's neck,

I inhale the sweetness of the fragrance
released by my strides through the swale,

and listen to the lucid notes
of a warbler's song honey the air.

Threshold

When he remembers the beginning, he looks
out the front windows of the cabin to the hills

and the colors of autumn this afternoon
in the sunlight, and thinks of her warmth,

her laughter. He remembers what was
beyond her smile, and thinking this

is all that matters: that continuum, that going
beyond they both enter, and a door

opens across another threshold,
where there is nothing but light, pure light.

Trailing Arbutus

I look for you intently, on my knees, among
drifted leaf litter near mountain summits, to find

your small, almost translucent, white petals,
blushing pink, barely open. Once, only

too common, you were sold on street corners
in Boston in the 1890s. Your shy flowers

are hidden beneath your rough, oval evergreen
leaves that too soon turn brown, but to have

inhaled your redolence is to know the sweet
excess of more than enough, why you are

also known as *the poet's flower.*
Little flower of irony, impatient to bloom

even before the last patches of snow begin
to melt, you are too quick to vanish.

Taking It Back with Me

I take the bracing cold down with me
from the fire tower at Mount Toby's summit.

I take the quality of the light with me —
its gold polish and September clarity;

the flash of those steel girders,
the breadth of the view: Monadnock's

granite dome just a touch north-northeast,
Greylock's prominence due west,

Snow's jagged peak at eleven o'clock.
I take the sound of the wind with me,

the invisible surf spreading
through treetops across this valley.

I stand on the wooden platform
of the top tier, my hands holding

onto a bend in the metal guardrail,
the Connecticut River flowing below,

swollen after days of rain, and before
taking it back with me, I watch

that one red oak leaf above the tree line,
suspended and spinning in the cross drafts.

Roaring Brook

The running luminescence
    of the sluice unwinding
        down the pudding-stone slope,

laced with white foam,
    creating one s after another;
        the word *silver* nearly audible

in the sound of its rush;
    the splash and churn
        at each bend and cascade.

Slanted beams of sunlight
    filling its effervescence and every pool;
        the effluence pouring

out of the culvert;
    the sound of the flow of what is infinite,
        framed in the moment,

or of, say, just being able
    to glance at all that is written
        on the long wall of the *akasha*.

The sounds of the water
    falling down the mountain,
        sliding from consonance

to assonance so many times
    they entwine to become the spool
        of a spoken word, voice itself, fluidity.

Living in the Moment

It is in knowing which particular
mineral is the one to take home
to mark this day's hike up the mountain

that might grace the *kata*
on the mantel of the fireplace
or one of the cabin's pine windowsills.

It is in choosing among the gleam
of quartz and the glistening of mica
as to what may remind you of the wind

in your ears at the summit.
It is in sensing a presence
in the clearing at dusk before

the snort of the startled doe's breath
clouds beneath the gibbous moon,
and its hooves clatter over the stones.

Mount Toby, Spring Thaw

The trickle of melting ice
catches in the basin beneath the culvert,
flows ledge to ledge, then descends

the stony bed worn between the banks
of the gorge. Runoff flashes
along the shoot of the frozen falls —

the thaw of the brook pausing
across a long table of snow-encrusted rock
before it tumbles over the rim of another.

The sluice slides down the doglegs
of ice, spills ribbons of water that plunge
through the beams of sunlight illuminating

each pool, and where, mid-mountain,
I stop to watch the rippling
water shadows silver the mossy cliffs.

My Death

The pigeons fly up past windowpanes
to the rooftops, then beyond

the rooftops. Pigeons fly up, not doves.
The dirge of traffic grinds to a stop.

Someone tries to rub a cinder from an eye,
and so much sunlight streaks

the brownstones a comforting rust.
This is it, the perpetuity of it all,

as I look up at the sheer face
of these cliffs, suddenly bright with patches

of moss and wild with the shaggy white
petals of wood asters.

What I have become is this
emptiness that rests within the cusp

of an open semicircle
embraced by fronds of maidenhair.

Roaring Falls: Mid-March

The stream rushes in sunlight
and a smell of decay rises through mist
that blows across drifted banks of snow.

Hiking the mountain to the falls, I pause,
listen to water flowing over stones.
A white birch trunk revolves in the rhythm

of an eddy in the basin below, the roar
of plunging water patterned within
ripples of the pool, within rings

of the tree itself; and here it's refoliated —
the spray of the falls, melting, refreezing —
along its branches, the clear icy leaves.

Listening to Rilke

He says that my mother's death
spreads out in both directions: to a point

that was and a point that will be.
I am fifty, he says, but

the eight-year-old in me stands
behind me in the shadow I cast

like a son who defers to his father.
He tells me he has begun

to make me believe that my actions
resemble those of a man who has

broken through something inside of himself.
His is the voice inside me that asks:

How aware are you? and says
There is no time, when I stand

in patches of sunlight that shine
through the forest canopy where

I listen to the rush of the brook
fall down the mountain slope,

and watch wave after wave of wind
break in the trees, whose sound

cleanses me like nothing else.
Rainer, my friend, one of my angels,

how ardently I listen to you,
as on the darkest of nights

when I walk for hours among
the snowy pages of your poems,

whose words glow like ingots
in the moonlight. In a dream,

when you appear to me, I have
needed to shield my eyes from

the cloud of light that surrounds you.
When I listen to the panther

you saw in the Jardin des Plantes
pace in its cage, sometimes, I too,

can feel my hands move beneath me,
as they write. How much I know

how difficult it is to revise
my life. What it is to remember,

at twenty, after first discovering
your poems, how I would stand out on

the library steps at dusk, one after another
for many dusks, and choose a star

burning above a dark doorway, filled
with awe of what it is *to be a beginner*

and *always having to begin.*
Sometimes when I am listening to you,

I become happy enough to stop to look up
on the mountain trail to identify

the trees by the shape of their leaves:
tulip, pignut hickory, white oak, sassafras,

and striped maple, then be able,
from a far-ranging cliff, to inhale

the fragrance of the hayed fields
below, the sweetness rising.

Kisses

Is the reason why I climb the trail up
the mountain to be reminded of her body,

to breathe in the scent of cinnamon
released in one shaft of sun after another

from the ferns that lie beyond?
When I am reminded of the fragrance

of her body, why do I imagine a trail
of smoke, as from an offering of incense,

taper upward, before it disappears
into the light? And why is it

after I place kisses over her body,
I inhale the redolence of ferns

on the mountain trail before
we leave the bed to rise in the morning?

Ode to Squash Soup

I strip the skin
        from the curves
                of butternut squash

with a paring knife;
        with the butcher knife,
                slice them in half;

take a soupspoon,
        remove the pulp and seeds;
                halve them again,

then halve the cubes,
        and set them aside.
                I peel potatoes,

scrub carrots, then dice them.
        I crush a bulb of garlic
                with the back of my hand,

and supply it
        to the chicken stock
                I pour into the pot;

immerse the vegetables;
        let them simmer.
                The windows mist,

the broth thickens.
        I add bay leaves;
                white pepper; rosemary,

for earthy fragrance;
        a touch of dry vermouth.
                I puree this in the blender,

then grate *Parmesan*
        for flavor. I ladle
                myself a bowl,

and before I dip my spoon,
        I taste the soup's sweetness
                in the steam rising.

March Wind

It blows loose brush and leaves into the air
across the opening of the field. Walk into it

and it tugs at your jacket, brushes back your hair.
It reawakens you to the persistent cold of winter,

despite your seeing spring in shoals of snowdrops
breaking through a crust of late snow.

It assuages you by its bitterness,
knifes through your layers: what your lover said,

then what she did, clarifies your aloneness.
It reminds you that the future is incalculable.

It begins to make you ready
to accept what is revealed in what is difficult.

It howls every time
it cuts loose the sorrow that weighs down the past.

Blue

In the photograph, the dress
my mother is wearing is periwinkle blue,

the pumps she has slipped into
a powder blue. The boutonniere

pinned to one of the lapels
of my father's beige suit is slate blue.

The steadfast eyes of my mother and father
are a discernible blue.

They stand in front of my father's Woody
on their wedding day.

The polished wood on its sides
contrasts the shades of blue

in the browned photograph.
The Woody's chrome and hubcaps sparkle.

Its burgundy hood and fenders shine.
Even the silver clouds suspended

in the gunmetal sky augur the intimations
of a color as blue as cerulean.

Neither one dreamed she would collapse,
or he would be consumed by drifting

deeper into the emptiness of a smoky blue haze.
The thought never occurred to them

my father would bury my mother,
and that he would not remember her

ever wearing that brocaded dress
and blue satin shoes.

The Use of Natural Objects

For a year after my mother died,
my father wore a black armband,

and the cold surrounded us.
I was unable to remember the last time

I saw her, when she walked me
to school on the first day of third grade.

Afterwards, she climbed the several
sets of concrete steps up the steep

slope to the apartment, then scaled
the three flights of stairs to where

she collapsed on the floor.
The year my mother died, my father

assisted me with a school project
that required the use of natural objects.

We constructed an Eskimo village
out of eggshells and cotton, a diorama

of igloos in a shoe box, my father's
black armband riding his biceps,

as we worked our gloveless
fingers in the cold surrounding us.

If It Is Meant to Be

That first Sunday in Whately, a cabbage white floats
beyond us, as if our energy together is the wind itself.

We talk about learning how to play "Silver Bells"
on the piano, so we can sing it at Christmas.

When you ask, *What is your favorite piece?*, both
of us choose the pleasing simplicity of the celadon

Chinese bowl; the Turkish candelabra, ornamented
with gilt-leaved loops around each candlestick

that open with the signature of infinity; the three
duodecimal volumes bound in the sensuality

of 15th-century Italian vellum. We walk in our own
sweet music, that easy wind that makes the pleats

of your skirt swirl, causes the creases of my slacks
to ripple. You see me in the shells in the bell jar

on the ledge of your office window.
When Rilke speaks about his hands, as he writes,

having a life of their own, you go on beyond me
somewhere, and I know I am a happy part of you.

Great Blue

When the great blue heron appears
　　through the leaves of the trees lining
　　　　the banks of the Farmington River,

I think of all that is marginal
　　in this life compared to those
　　　　slow, powerful wings, rowing the air

above the river's heart.
　　The plumed head looks to the left,
　　　　then to the right, as it cranes to peer

into the water of the river's
　　swift current, cresting its banks,
　　　　flowing with the rush of the insistent

June rain. And I think of you,
　　and wish you had been beside me
　　　　to see the great bird, that sacred vision,

rowing the air, and searching
　　the heart of the river. So, I think, is
　　　　this why I am alive, that being with you

is like stepping into the sunlight
　　after days of rain, and to know that
　　　　you are opening in ways you have never

opened before? I think,
　　as the great blue heron flies
　　　　out of sight, that I row the air above

the river of your heart, neither of us
        being able to comprehend those powerful
                wings, unable to gauge that the vision

of the epiphanal would be a reason
        anyone standing on the banks would
                want to break into song, and might

even propel the heron further into
        following the strong current of you,
                surging past the low-hung tendriled leaves.

Radiance

Over your gray and white oval marble-top kitchen table,
the meeting of our eyes makes the room grow brighter.
Our faces, layer after layer, face after face,

become so vibrant, the light appears to crest in waves.
We have become changed by it, nothing can be
the same after it. When I bend down to touch

the shape of deer tracks in the damp sand, it is in
the same way I place my fingers over your body.
When I stand beside a freshet in a meadow

the sun catches the rings of the water's long ripples
in the wind, that is the same glimmer we hold
when our eyes meet in the kitchen over

your gray and white oval marble-top table.
Every day for the rest of my life, yours is the face
I want to see when I awake in the morning.

Moving the Woodpile

I am rinsed in quiet living here in this cabin in the woods,
and move the woodpile this September afternoon to make room

for a clothesline between white pine and sugar maple.
Clearing the skids of wood, I discover a white-footed mouse,

who blinks, then bounds off through years of fallen leaves;
a black salamander who wriggles deeper into bark mulch;

wolf spiders who display, if not demand, their presence;
stinkbugs who drive themselves in circles like bumper cars;

and a leopard frog who jumps, then leaps, disturbing
a swath of snakeskin *rubbed off against the bark.*

I restack the wood on the skids, then chink in the splits.
When the sky clouds over, and my sweat beads on the wood,

it is filigreed with the gills of beige and white mushrooms.
After I rake that spot of chipped bark and slivers,

sunlight bolts between the leaves, and shines on cleared earth,
then lights on the newly stacked wood.

Putting Up the Mailbox

I pull up the twisted jack pine post
with gloved hands, surprised to find

I need to jerk the cinderblock
it is attached to out of the ground,

where it leaned on one side for years.
I mallet the new metal base two feet deep

with the back-edge of an axe.
The echo of my pounding on the target

2 by 4 in the center ricochets through
the woods on either side of the road.

Ravens lift above the trees to begin
their wonk-wonk, and with each swing

I am jolted into a joy of hammering.
After I snap down the metal locks

at the base with the strokes of a hammer,
I place the four-foot-tall milled pine post

into it, then center the white pine platform
on top, drive in wood screws to secure

the new box on both sides and in back,
then bank the base with the stones

I unearthed, and fill in the old spot with dirt.
I walk around it, to admire its height,

its straightness, its square to the road.
Now when I check the mail, I open the lid,

knowing I erected what is durable,
and raised what is reliable in myself.

Cinnamon Sticks

You asked me years ago, *Tell me how you know when to use them?*
I do not remember what I answered you then, but it is
in their aromatic sweetness and their pungence that they can
achieve piquancy in a dish. It can be in a simple curry,

or in a *Bolognese.* Stir the cinnamon sticks in with extra-virgin
olive oil in a pan over the flame, several dashes of coriander,
cumin, Garam Masala, a whole bulb of crushed garlic, diced
sweet Mayan onion, chopped Holland and green bell peppers.

Then add crushed tomatoes, tomato paste, a pound
of uncooked ground beef—the sliced zucchini goes in last—
and love, yes, an ingredient of love, over low heat for an hour,
although it is the last component in the concoction that

neither one of us will ever forget. Seeing you standing
at the crosswalk the other day, as I did just happen to drive
past, when we both waved and smiled, made me think
of your asking me about cinnamon sticks, and how I can

finally offer you an answer specific enough, in that
I use them the same way I would massage those knots loose
in the muscles of your back, then place kisses on each
of your bare shoulders. It occurred to me that I use

cinnamon sticks just that way, although I did think about
another question you would ask me, which was, *I want to know
what those lights are when I look at you; what are those lights,
and where do they come from?* After all these years of our being

separate from one another, but together being able to enter
ever further into the light of what is beatific, that shines
from each of our faces, it appears through this radiance
we have become aware of that question having answered itself.

from

Blessing and Homage

(2012)

Franklin Merrell-Wolff

Wolff, as you may begin to endearingly call him,
fashions one tautological sentence after another.

You can imagine each sentence diagrammed
on a chalkboard to illustrate their precision.

The ontological nature of Wolff's teaching
parallels the eighth century Buddhist sage, Shantideva,

who, after giving his discourse on emptiness,
The Bodhicharyavatara, the Bodhisattva levitated,

then disappeared. However, Wolff remains
Wolff, and transcends Wolff at the same time.

His vigorous noetic ponderings, more than just
philosophical pyrotechnics, approximate mathematical

formula, a language that points toward the heavens
within oneself and the ineffable radiance there.

It is in the "Third Recognition," and his writing of *felicity*,
Wolff posits the loss of self as *Consciousness without*

an Object, and even before relinquishing the concept,
you may hear a beneficence of spirit as a kind of singing.

The Geese

Tonight, geese cut off from their flock
pass close above my head in thick fog.

I lift up my voice in song,
and call to them by way of greeting.

I am surprised when they begin to follow me
through the air as I walk in the fog

toward the cloud of glare showered
from the spotlight on the side of the barn.

Each one answers the honking
of the other and my singing, as they circle

in the light, before they regroup and continue
on their journey. Long after they have faded

in the distance, once again, alone,
now in the silence, I am filled with their voices.

Ode to February

Sweet onions and sardines browned in a skillet in olive oil,
served with the blessing of two day-old baguette and a glass

from a bottle of an affordable Cotes-Du-Rhone, is the closest
I may ever come to *Tushita Heaven*, as I listen to the pouring

winter rain, and am aware I need little else that compares
with *just this* and these blue lights that flash in their nests

of snow shadow from the slow moving traffic I watch
from the front windows of the farmhouse that face the road.

Bloodroot Open before Trillium

Whatever it was I lost, whatever I wept for
Was a wild, gentle thing, the small dark eyes
Loving me in secret.
    James Wright

Last of the snow melt
        drips from the sodden, mossy cliffs —
            yellow bands of sunlight stippling

the fresh spring greens.
        Water sound rises from the gorge —
            the brook tumbling down the slope

before it races over boulders
        at the chute of the falls. The wet air
            rinsing my face with its sound.

Beside the mountain trail,
        muddy with runoff, the race
            of the brook quickens into a pool,

and I am reminded
        of my Grail Castle experience
            when I was thirteen, so like Parsifal,

woods-walking for the first time
        alone, how I sensed *those hidden eyes loving*
            me in secret, James Wright speaks of.

As I hike through the shadows
        of new leaves, the path to the summit
            is littered on both sides with birch,

beech, and hemlock, uprooted after
        the ice storm last December, chain-sawed
            into slash — resin still burning the air.

Backlit in a Wash of Light

for Art Goodtimes

I think of you writing me last night,
   of your grief. The invisible lead filling
      the interstices between your words:

I'm in San Francisco.
   My brother is dying. It's been
      nearly thirty years since we hiked up

Slaughterhouse Gulch, when you were
   living at the foot in the pine lodge,
      where legend has it Butch Cassidy

practiced jumping onto his horse
   before he robbed the San Miguel
      Valley Bank in Telluride, and rode

out of that box canyon in 1889.
   A mourning cloak leads me, then
      shadows me, on the path, not unlike

you playing *Coyote* back then. We lassoed
   ropes onto the rocky outcrops above
      dry waterfalls on our way to the top

of the mesa that was studded orange
   with poppies, where I watched you
      stalk a herd of elk, before we hiked

back down to recross the shallow race
   of that part of the Colorado River.
      Here, on Mount Toby in western

Massachusetts, just beyond
     pine shade and leaf-mold, the petals
          of trailing arbutus begin to flower —

some buds open, others closed;
     all so new among their quickly
          browning leaves. I'm still inhaling

the sweetness of their fragrance
     even after having almost descended
          the trail — then just happen to look

back up the mountain
     slope to see spray from
          the brook backlit in a wash of light.

Blessing

A pair of mourning cloaks drift among the white flowers
of wood anemones and the runners of blossoming wild strawberry.

Fiddleheads begin to unfurl on the slopes,
and trillium, nearly gone past, now resembles its nickname,

Stinking Benjamin, its dried and wrinkled
three-pointed boutonnieres having been pollinated by flies.

On the dusty April trail, far too dry for this time of the year,
a horse's hooves have fractured stones along the path

that litter the rise to the summit, leaving some of them
broken in the shape of a heart. Clusters of Quaker Ladies,

in shoals of blue petals, amid their golden yellow centers,
ripple beside the trailside in a rush of wind. Hillside

after hillside of new foliage, not quite green, begins to leaf out
across the breadth of forest, sloping over the ridges, among

the pines, from the view at the fire tower from Greylock
to Monadnock. Creaking in the wind like the unoiled iron hinges

of a barn door, and returning back into the nothingness
from which it came, a raptor's call issues across an amethyst sky.

Tone Poem for Summer Solstice

after Robert Francis

Say oxeye daisy tansy yarrow orange hawkweed
purple clover Say skipper mourning cloak silver-

bordered fritillary monarch clouded sulfur Say
blue-eyed grass blue toadflax ragged robin *rosa*

rugosa shinleaf *pyrola* jewelweed white campion
Say bluebird swallow purple martin Say dragonfly

honey bee bald-faced hornet Say downy brome
curly dock barnyard grass hop clover Say warbler

Summer Palette

after the paintings of Shirley Fredrickson Conant
and her Burnett Watercolor Show, March 2010

The resplendent summer immemorial of Down East flora
and clean Edward Hopper-plumb lines of roof and sill,

with the opacity of windows filled with light,
with the clarity of windows reflecting a particular patch

and specific hue of sky, draw us into the periphery
of the landscapes that the artist has chosen for us to walk into.

My favorite, "Blueberry Basket," painted
in Sedgwick, Maine, brims its near-overflow with Taoist

sensibilities, succulent with the delectable fruit
of the highbush shrubs that fringe the meander

of the middle path in an *homage* to the pastels of summer.
The daisies, cinquefoil, and beach plum that flowers

and ripens in each of these canvasses, is an illuminated page
in the wordless Book of Odes in celebration of the rock-ribbed

Maine coast that opens to us with the fragrance of the sea
breeze, with the dunes awash in *rosa rugosa*,

where the Bonsai of rock reflects rock in the ocean
of a single puddle, where the needles of a crooked pine mirror

a forest in the pools of low tide, quaking with
petals of lupine that speckle the ripples and flash in the dusk.

Cinnamon and Honey

after Wolfgang Amadeus Mozart's
Clarinet Concerto in A, Kochel 622

We have lived most of our lives
Preparing for what it is

We think we have lost —
Before beginning to just come into

Our knowing how the fulfillment
Of consciousness unfolds

Into its own sumptuousness,
Whose pleasure supreme

Offers a similar taste as that of cinnamon,
And how much and how often

We can possibly spread the silkiness
Of its lusciousness through emanations

Through and around us,
Flowing like honey from a broken comb,

Like the light irradiating its flow,
And the color of the light imbued

With the honey, and the sweetness
Beyond just a honeyed sweetness,

When the light emanates not only
Around us any sunny morning,

As the walls of the red brick brownstones
Sparkle in a steady stream,

But also swells through us in a confluence
As a river that flows into the sea.

Gyuto Monks

for Robert Spiess

chanting Gyuto monks —
an aroma beyond
the fragrance of incense

sparkling in the mind . . .
      the Gyuto monks'
ringing of bells

each monk's face —
the light of the deity
emanating through it

chanting Gyuto monks
      . . . an inner eye
opens wide

in saffron and yellow robes —
Gyuto monks fill the air
with chanting

intoning three tones into one:
      the resonant choir
of Gyuto monks

Quiet

When the house is this quiet,
the refrigerator sings.

Silence crouches in a dusty corner.
You can hear it crack its knees.

My ears begin drumming.
I hear a voice whisper:

Listen to the air.
Listen to the air breathe. Listen . . .

It's only the wind—
a dying man's breath

rapping on the windows,
cold knuckles of the autumn breeze.

from

Velocity

(2013)

After Having Stacked the Cord the Day Before

I gather the larger scraps
    for kindling this morning of frost,
        then rake the wood chips across

the rutted driveway dirt
    and over the shoulder into scrub pines.
        I carry the unearthed rocks caught

in the rake's tines to the clearing
    where the garden flourished.
        I set the rake down, free the rubble

from the prongs, and let
    an inner pair of hands
        (initially, I resist) guide mine

as I erect several cairns,
    each a few inches high, find
        the center of balance in each stone,

a harmony of grooves
    in each face. Along the embankment
        above the brook, wind combs through

the stand of beech. A *hosanna*
    of notched leaves cascades across
        each wave, the crevice of each ripple.

Cushman Brook, Early October

I am washed by the brook's sound,
spreading out over its bed of stones.

I come to an opening,
this freedom to flow, to deepen

in my own channel, and watch
ribbons of water plunge

over a table of rock —
how sunlight falls on the rivulets

that rush around an outcrop,
then spill into the clarity of a pool.

The Gingko

We anticipated that day in autumn, for the precise instant
its leaves would fall at once, all those papery yellow fans

still attached to the gingko's limbs. They fell
in a delicate golden flurry. Spinning in a single gust,

they flew like dervishes, like flames. A carillon rang
from the bell tower, struck chimes vibrating on the wind,

leaves scattering a trail across the skim ice
of the small pond, in the frozen wake of rippled water —

leaving the tree lit in our minds,
sunlight flooding through the leafless branches.

The Pendulum

I watch the first juncos, those augurs
of winter, flock after late October snow

in their charcoal gray feathers,
as if they just emerged out of the ashes

of a hearth, their beaks the color of pale flame.
I think of us that first autumn —

how you laugh before you toss back your hair,
how we bask in the light

that emanates between us —
how deep we walk into and out of what

we think we want, how I try to find a way
to still the pendulum of our going

back and forth the same way again.
I walk the pine floors of this cabin in the woods

where I hear your voice, saying:
Why haven't other people written about this?

This is where I weather the irony
of your being unable to accept what you told me

that you waited for all of your life.
This is where I learn to cease grieving.

The Language of Our Hands

How strong expression is when indicated
with the language of our hands.

Always fresh from the old country,
my grandmother rubbed the index finger

of one hand up and down lengthwise
and perpendicular to the index finger

of the other. The fingers busied themselves
over each arthritic joint.

They cleaned off something grimy that sticks,
pointed to the shame of the *little butter thief*

for not eating the food placed before him.
I squirmed with embarrassment by just what

such a sign might suggest, or whenever
this gesture was made for not always cleaning

my plate, that often held me captive, especially
on Fridays, by a fish with an unblinking eye.

For Walt Whitman

You contain all men and all women because of the cosmos
That you are. Not your face alone, and not your walk alone,
Not your touch alone, and not your presence alone,
Not your essence alone, and not that I can comprehend
Or understand your essence, or your essence *en masse*,
Although you are ubiquitous, you are democratic.
I recognize you in the wrinkles of the faces of the old;
And, yet it is your healthy sense of *Puer aeternus* that inspires
An appetite for abandon. It is your touch that I feel
When I sweep my hand through clover; and yet become
Aware of your prickly individuality when I brush my fingers
Over thorns on the stems of roses. Your essence, I propose,
Is like my essence, not that I can comprehend or understand
My essence, or any solitary particle of my essence, or any
Solitary particle of your essence, but what is essence
If it is not in all people, in all places, and in all things; yet you
Are unlike anyone I have ever known, because of the breadth
Of your songs regarding the grass that we love; and since
I am uncertain whether it is you that takes one of my hands
In yours, in a celebration of exuberance, or whether it is me
That reaches out to you to place one of your hands in mine.

Practicing Mindfulness

1   All day the rain blows in gusts; mist moves in
to swirl above the crackling of fallen leaves,
to fill the branches of the trees where their foliage

had been, then disappears, reappears; the wind
driving browned pine needles through the air.
I cartwheel the rotted skids I cleared

a hundred feet down the slope behind the cabin,
then lay out the new pine skids I acquired
from the lumber yard *for free.*

2   I practice mindfulness in moving
the split wood onto the skids: at first one piece
in either hand, then I develop carting

an armload, the grit from the wood
muddying my work gloves, and the rain
falling hard enough that I change hats

from my beret to Provincetown ball cap.
I stack the wood on the three skids
farthest from the cabin four feet high;

the skid I place closest to the front door,
I stack higher. Sometimes a knot in a piece
of split wood looks back at me like an eye,

and I move through the mist and pelting rain
all afternoon to finish just before darkness —
only the slash of the pile remaining.

Outside the Box

If you hadn't been privy to observe
her transformation over the years, then you couldn't easily

discern that she had the change executed and met
the challenge of becoming transgender. Her courage

is what offered me most resilience, that steadfastness
in face of what the world might have thought about

her choosing. I would need to summon my own courage
when I was unfairly terminated and would no longer walk

down the hill to the parking lot due to bullyism on the job
that was all too similar to the Nazi *Beer Hall Putsch* —

the malicious smile of the new store director
and the *machismo* and *machisma* of his henchmen,

the bottomless stupidity in their eyes in their buddying-up
to exercise the fascism of the corporation,

the philosophy of there being no thoughts outside the box.
That reminded me of when I was ganged up on

and beaten in the sandbox, as a child,
by some of the other boys who flexed their naked bravado,

how after I was pummeled with fists
I would try to stand up and spit out the dirt in my mouth.

Left Unsaid

While I am still here I will open the front windows
To allow the late August coolness to enter the room.

I will sit in a chair beside the dining room table
With the maroon tablecloth and celebrate

My gratefulness with a simple breakfast of peanut
Butter and peach preserve on toast, a glass of orange

Juice, and iced coffee. I will look out at the orb
Weaver webs strung out among the dew of the grass;

And watch the garter snake, that has grown so much
Since last summer, and who lives under the side porch,

Sun on the bricks of the walk. While I am still here,
I will walk in the morning sunlight, and experience

Myself as one with all, as I look out over
The Pelham Hills, still blanketed with remnant wisps

Of vestigial mist. I will accept that which is within
Myself, and come to terms with my having nursed

The urge of hanging a rope up in the barn
And stepping off a chair. For reasons left unsaid,

I will make use of the day every way I can,
While I am still here.

Sunshower

To watch the shower move down
the length of the street, and continue,

made me aware the gift given to me
was stepping outside just then to witness

the rain darkening the asphalt, to observe
the line between wet and dry diminish

until the rain reached me, and in its wake,
to inhale the olfactory stimulant

of ionized air. That such a natural event
inspires a child's laughter, and distinguishes

itself as a perfect oxymoron, is
testimony to its definition, especially after

I return inside, to savor prismed raindrops
beading the lenses of my glasses.

from

Invocation

(2015)

A Field of Sunflowers

La tristesse durera toujours.
          Vincent van Gogh

Give up what you want to gain,
     the guide says, as I pass a field
          of sunflowers, the inflorescence of all of the flower

heads facing east to greet
     the sun; and the one stalk in the rear
          of the field a corolla-head higher than the rest, making

an offering of itself, as did
     the Buddha, by holding up a single flower,
          as I find within myself a smile that spreads outward,

similar to Mahakasyapa's smile that
     traced the recognition of true *Self* across his lips.
          Whether seeming a slight of hand, that magician's trick

of heliotropism, with each sympetalous
     face, a throng of spiritual devotees turns
          to the sun in unison, alert to the silent *Mullah* calling

the rising of the light. Their flower heads
     are the faces of those just after morning prayers
          before they rise from their knees beneath the mosque

of blue sky to choose not to enter into
     another day of *Jihad*, and they resemble
          the faces of those who begin their day in the same fields,

who blend into the marketplace,
     in the midst of the sweetness of their lives,
          that make a choice to ignite the truck bomb, to detonate

the IED, and as *saboteurs*, whether
    to pull the cord on their suicide belt while standing
        beside the flower seller's stall. One raft after another

of sunflowers, head to stem, floating
    on their roots, was used to mop up the nuclear spill
        at Chernobyl. Although Vincent, poor man, chose to

perish as he strode through a field
    of *Helianthus*, as he clutched at the canvasses
        he had painted of them, and in placing those paintings

down among a row, aimed a pistol at his chest,
    with what we might imagine as trembling
        hands, then pulled the trigger, wounding himself mortally.

Two days later, he died at the Inn at Ravoux,
    not only among the beauty emanating from each
        of their bright faces, but also amid their brilliant splendor.

Montepulciano and Caravaggio

I have thought about you tonight in my savoring a glass, or two,
of a delicious Montepulciano D'Abruzzo (Vendemmia 2008),

along with a double-cream Brie. However, it would have been
better paired with a Gorgonzola, but I am not complaining.

This particular Montepulciano offers such a rich palette
of various layers of dark cherry, and spice laced with purple plum,

that open out across the tongue, and in tasting it I imagine
I could be viewing a still life by Caravaggio, and concomitantly

sharing in the portion of the abundance spread
across the table in the light from beyond the edges of the painting.

The last sentence is an example of what is known as paratactic
syntax, that is sometimes attributed to the adaptation

of Oriental poetry in English, in which two dissimilar
images, or fragments, are juxtaposed without any direct connection

of one statement with the other, such as: It is snowing tonight,
and I will step into the storm to sit beneath the white candelabra

of the branches of the Kousa dogwood. Perhaps a better example is:
Tomorrow I will walk across the snowy fields, and when I stop

by the river in the sunlight, I will think of Caravaggio
and taste the Montepulciano I drank last night

but not the Gorgonzola I did not complain being without,
since I deferred to my humility, and left it in the painting.

Black-eyed Susan

Butter-yellow inflorescence, ballerina's skirt
ruffled in the wind, common sweetheart

of wildflowers, who eschews the solitary
for a throng of other Susans; the brown,

dark-purplish center one of summer's
most obvious, most subtle of baubles.

Double Gold, Indian Summer, Marmalade,
your various shades reveal your inimitable

humor. Leaning wildly windward,
rising in a stand, resting together in the sun,

the summer's lushness no longer lush without
your strong-stemmed, unconstrained bounty —

solstice celebrant, resplendent
Susan among so many Susans.

Experiencing the Light

Then there were the mornings, when I would set
the table for breakfast and your cat would talk to me

in her feline language of meows, of happy yowls, before
you came down the stairs, and we would smile. It was

at that time you nicknamed me Mr. Man, the one who
spoke with your cat, the one with whom you could

confide in when you might see a window-paned wall
as stained glass, or the time we saw the heron's aura

in the sky above us while picnicking in a hayed summer
meadow. What I will remember best is the light

that emanates and haloes both our faces when we are
together and we let it. What I will always miss

is unbuttoning your blue cardigan, the softness of it,
that opened to the hardness of nipples, and how

I understood what it was to love the body of a woman
after having been with other women over many years,

for the first time. Each time was a nuptial, and every time,
those moments lapsed into their own perpetuity,

like the beatific smoothness of the marble
of a Michelangelo, and the light sculpted in Mary's face

in *La Pieta*, in the creation of something other than
the sculpture itself, there was the light we entered

that our bodies could not exhaust — even the fragrance
of your sweat was sweet to me. What our bodies did

to each other, when you still used to grant them that
blissful abandon, was a revelation beyond prayer.

What I did to break the crystal that held the clarity
of what we held and what held us was my own fear

of breakage, my inadequacy of living in the eternity
of the moment. What humility I have learned, and at

what cost, after having been taught that lesson, I now
know how I could not have lost you, but lost you I have.

When on those occasions we see each other, only by
my own inventive making, it is the ring of our laughter

together that fills any room. It is in experiencing
the light beginning to fill each other's face that makes me

think how easy it would have been to have made
this work each day of our lives, but we would have

needed to have grounded our experience in the divinity
of the everyday, and I believe it is in our seeking

divinity everyday that we have not only lost the art
of being together but also the practice and the path. It is

by your saying that simple yes to me when I suggest to you
that what we have had has lasted without lasting.

Wild Falling

Eyes frozen in headlights for
only a moment, the herd

of deer traverses the road
in this first winter blizzard

with such prudence they quiet
the wild falling. One after

another, they spring to clear
the ice-sheathed barbed wire hurdle,

that quivers from time to time
when one of their hooves grazes

against it. They bound into
the meadow, filling with white

fire, an icy afterglow
burnishing their tracks, that cross

and re-cross themselves, while wisps
of cloud wash over the moon.

Rilkean Dream

I dreamed of myself as a light following
A greater series of lights, in a particular
Pattern of circles —

A veritable sense of a spiritual
Architecture, as in the shell of a conch,
Or what is sonic in the soaring arcs

Of language —
What Rilke's monk exhibits
In his painting —

Brushing the luminous colors
Of the ineffable in words.
Transcendence isn't tangible, or tacit,

But a glimmering,
As a ray of light, or the single wave
In one ripple of water after another.

Satori

for Robert Jones

Yes, it has been long enough. It has been long enough that hearing
from you this evening is much like having stepped onto what is

apparently an unfamiliar subway car, and in a moment of the terrific
velocity of G-force, I find myself, years later, sitting at my worktable

here in my studio near the foot of Long Mountain in South Amherst,
Massachusetts, writing you. I especially appreciate your emailing

the photograph of you standing beside Robert Spiess, who is wearing
the medal from his having been presented with the Shiki Award,

and holding open the bound citation in his hands. You are correct
in your assessment that he was in league with Emerson and Mencken,

as an editor. Anyone can see what the award meant to him by
his facial expression and body language. Did you know that he was

a surrogate father to me? Thank you for the update on your Lavelle
translations — I appreciate that. Louis Lavelle being the Christian

mystic of the *intelligentsia*, in direct opposition to
    Sartre's existentialism.
The Act of Presence is a text I look forward to rereading.
    Could it be that

I remember studying Lavelle all those years ago? I feel that, through
you, the universe touched me on the shoulder this evening, and I am

grateful that you precipitated my own *presence* in a
    deeply-experienced
satorial flash — just in an instant. D. T. Suzuki wrote: *Satori*
    is the raison

d'être of Zen, without which Zen is no Zen. You reminded me of
    the truth
of who I am, where my eternal home is, here or elsewhere: *in the*
    moment.

Vixen

Here on the farm the vixen
    hunts during the day; how
        exquisitely she moves, how beautifully

fox-red, whenever she breaks off
    the language of her body that intends
        never to be seen. Last Sunday, I crossed

over to the windbreak
    of leafless trees, among the hummocks
        that descend into the drainage ditch beyond

where she was tracking,
    unaware of my immediacy, within a few
        yards, so mindful was she of mice, of rats

in the matted stalks of the meadow.
    This afternoon, she emerged
        in the clearing beyond the barn. I watched

her stretch and shake
    luxuriously, so unconstrained
        after a day and night of winter rain. Now,

she begins to trail
    a new scent, nose down
        among the dark roots of the browned grass.

Sinewed, she articulates open
    ground on black-furred feet —
        a streak of flame igniting the wind, a mind

at one in the conflagration
  of the moment, shoulders
    hunched, arched hair on neck, her vernacular

perpetual patrol
  and reconnaissance,
    her sudden disappearance only an exhibition

of her sudden reappearance,
  her reappearance the command parlance
    of her disguise among what is apparent in

her inexorable leap,
  pouncing on a meadow vole,
    or whatever stirs beneath her, as our hearts

quicken, her saliva-flecked tongue
  flashing, the tail of her succulent prey
    brandished between the wedge of her jaws.

In the Shade of a Cave

We hike halfway up Mount Toby to where the gorge drops
off and takes the thin stream of Roaring Brook down

toward the culvert beneath train tracks to Cranberry Pond.
I explain that the water is normally roaring every spring

from the snowmelt; however, not having much of a winter
has affected the watersheds. I illustrate that usually

the force of the brook hammers the stones, that the sound
mixes with the ionization of the water rising above the cliffs,

so that you can see, hear, and smell the torrent all at once.
In giving Bob a guided tour of the flora bordering the trail

this mid-April, I find the Quaker Ladies grouped in blue
and white clusters at the bottom, in the scrub meadow that

overlooks the pond. Farther up where I warn him
that here is where the trail begins to become steep, I spot

one nodding purple trillium, then point out the others
blazing their own trail up the slope. He aims the camera

to shoot his photographs of what he describes
as their flowers *looking downward*, and I explain that is why

part of their name includes the word *nodding*. He tells me
that he was an infantryman in the Battle of the Bulge,

one of four soldiers out of a platoon of forty who survived
the surging storm troopers. I point to the bright yellow

discs of inflorescence of coltsfoot flourishing beside
a trickle of a stream cutting its way through the black mud.

There! I exclaim, and identify the four-lobed lush purple
flowers of hepatica, whose royal hues can be easily missed

due to their diminutive size among leaf litter. I speak
with an intended ebullient clarity that I hope he remembers

when we find the clearing beneath the mossy cliffs halfway
up the mountain, speckled white with the luscious

blossoming of bloodroot. I inform him that there is only
a two-week window of our seeing this perennial in the wild,

of which he shows his rapt appreciation by taking one
photograph after another. *Do you see that one*, I say, placing

one of his hands in one of mine, as I draw a straight line
to where one bloodroot flower grows in the shade of a cave

in the cliffs. Oh, I see, he answers, then continues:
Yesterday I couldn't feel my hands and feet from the trench foot I got

in the battle. They only gave us thin gloves, so we could fire our rifles.
My feet froze, since the boots they gave us were not much,

and the socks were too goddamn thin! We look at each other,
with mutual understanding beneath green cliffs, whose

natural architecture we both admire, among blossoms
of bloodroot that star the entire vertical rise in the sunlight.

Homage to Ed Ricketts

When you drove up Drake Avenue that evening, you had
Just spoken with your sister Alice over the phone.

Your last words to her being, *I have never been any happier*
In my entire life. You had just married a young woman,

You were only days away from leaving on another
Expedition to the Queen Charlotte Islands with Steinbeck

To write a book that was to be entitled *The Outer Shores.*
Was it your musing about the sea worm that distracted you?

Or was it the list of what you needed to pack
For the expedition? Did the rusted 1936 Packard stall

On the railroad tracks, as the Delmonte Express, on its way
From San Francisco, turned the blind curve from behind

One of the canneries, to bear down on you, as the engineer
Blew the whistle several times, before the train crashed

Into the car, carrying you down the tracks three hundred
Feet away, spilling you and the Packard off to the side?

The collision startled most of the saintly bums from
Their dreams at the foot of the hill along Cannery Row.

At that moment, Monterey would never be any quieter.
Nothing would ever be quite the same again.

John Steinbeck's Doc and Joseph Campbell's *Hero with*
A Thousand Faces would pass from this specific incarnation

Three days short of your fifty-first birthday. Described as
Having a face that was *part Christ, part satyr*, the wise voice

That everyone seemed to listen to was silenced because
Of either a stalled car or the distraction of your thinking

About the ecology of sardines, instead of paying attention
To an oncoming passenger train crossing an intersection

Without the safety of a wigwag. I imagine that you reside
In your own version of paradise: dawn at low tide on one

Of the most remote of the Queen Charlotte's, off the coast
Of British Columbia, the tidal flats spread out before you

For your prospecting of marine specimens, stretching out
In the bracing cold and the pink brightness of the new day —

The innumerable starfish dotting their universe over
The expanse of the abated Pacific tide, and you persevering

In the perpetuity of the perigee and the apogee in gathering
Nothing but grace from the abundance of the sea.

The Blind

Walking back from the mailbox on the roadside,
With junk mail in my hands, I think about

All of the letters from Catholic societies that
Were addressed to my mother after she died.

The letters often contained pendants devoted to
The Blessed Virgin, and all of them, I am sure,

Were petitions for donations. My response,
As a child, was: *Why didn't all of these people*

Know that my mother had died, why were they
Still sending her letters? Receiving those letters

Reminded me of the grief I would feel when
The blind would ring the buzzer on the front

Steps of our home, their stark white canes
Made only more isolate in the brightness

Of the sun. The blind would go door to door
To sell packets of needles, and I would always

Be startled by the obviousness of their loss,
The bleak unlit hallways their lives had become.

I recall one blind woman, with a spectrally
Beautiful face, whose pupils were occluded

With a milkiness, whom my mother purchased
Needles from, my mother the seamstress who

Could have provided the blind woman with
Sewing kits full of needles. A similar grief

Resonated within me when, after waiting for
The door to open, I was told that you weren't

In today, the stab of disappointment an arrow
Slowly quivering in me, despite my denials.

Being bereft is never censure to the heart
Opening, it is central to it, it is the key.

Apples

When I serve one of the apples I bought
On a white plate, sliced in quarters, then

Sliced again in thirds, along with a slice
Of cheese, it is an elegant meal unto itself,

Not necessarily breakfast, but a spare lunch,
With that always attractive combination

Of aesthetics and utility. The apples I chose
For this week were Cortlands, Macouns,

And Honey Crisps, each its own cadenza
In the symphony of streaming October

Sunlight, as strong as the light in Emmaus
When Christ reappeared to the disbelief

Of his apostles. Each apple, one for each
Day, as resilient as if it were its own last

Meal, as if we could ever plan a more perfect,
More impeccable last meal. The apples

I chose offered their own salient characteristics,
Such as the robustness of the Cortland, and

The crunch of the Macoun, and the sweetness
Of the Honey Crisp. Each bite its own taste

And texture. Each its own compliment
To the steady inflorescence of the October

Sunlight, with the sense of ending and
Beginning, with the aspect of the light of Christ

Already in our heart, with that heady fullness
Of our brimming over with the abundance

Of the fruit of the harvest, and in what is
The redolence of the fragrance of apples.

In Memory of Jack Gilbert

In my passing the herd of goats grazing the meadow
Adjacent to Little Creek Farm, I think of you, especially

In my seeing the male with his twisted horns crowning
His wizened head, the sunlight flickering between

The birches and the pines this morning as I drive north.
The baritone of the semis passing me going south with

Their diesel engines droning in the bluster of the wind
Shear as they blow by me. I compare your work to itself

As I compare Mozart's *Prague Symphony* driving up
To Petersham and then to his *Jupiter Symphony* driving

Back to Amherst. As you might write, the achievement
Is in the achieving, in the delight of eating the apple past

The seeds and the core, in loving a woman beyond
One's magisterial heart to find what it might be that draws

Us into deeper mystery when we move past ego
And adoration to the essence that is even further past

Lust and beauty. On our last hike together before you left
Fort Juniper to travel to your Greek mountain,

I joked about the plethora of mushrooms, newly sprouted
After the late summer rain, and how they were

Yet to be fully formed, reminding me of early drafts
Of poems, and you laughed. You possessed the wisdom

To teach gently, then fiercely; and to discern the difference
Between the two. With you now irrevocably gone,

I envision you prospering on your own hardscrabble island
Much like Prospero, the wind in your hair on a cliff above

The bright blue of the Aegean. Although your books will
Never be buried, at least not by you or those who have been

Nourished by them. Although what you might now hear,
Among the island's stony silences, may just sound similar

To the applause Prospero heard, in the cadence of waves
Crashing on the shore, releasing you from the bonds

Of the rigor of your own poems, which you so obstinately
Held to; of their ardor, which you offered to us as gifts;

As beacons in the night, in whose distant glow we steer
Toward, when each one of us dips the oars and begins

To row, headed for our own remote island, upon which
All the years of sorrow will be worth the yearning

Of our particular heart, for whatever reasons, that we will
Later discover, are why, at last, we have come.

Green Olives

I stood at the crest of the hill on the rock wall among
Stakes of barbed wire fence looking down at the cows

That grazed the rolling hillocks overlooking the city
Below, and remarked, *What abandon, what freedom.*

My friend, Darrell, responded, *You poet!* This was
The first time I had run away from home, from being

Locked out of the house for not wearing the ill-fitting
Wide wale corduroys. This was before I ran away

And acquired my first apartment, with an over-the-road
Truck driver who snored, when I was sixteen.

This was before I inadvertently broke the storm window
Of the screen door when I slammed it as I left for

My commute to morning classes of my freshman year
At college; both my father and stepmother continuing

To throw cups, plates, and their breakfast against
The dining room wall. This was before I returned

In the evening to policemen who arrested me
For breach of peace, before I spent the night in jail,

Before I had dropped out of school. When
I stood there at the crest of the hill, the entire world

Appeared to be spread out before me. Then Darrell
And I descended to the bottom to the white farm house

Where his grandmother lived. He told me she would
Make us lunch, and that his favorite part of lunch were

The green olives. We were served bologna sandwiches
With yellow mustard on white bread. Then Darrell's

Grandmother placed a whole jar of green olives stuffed
With pimento beside our two glasses of milk. I can still

Hear Darrell chew his sandwich with gusto, as I did mine;
And we consumed one olive, then a second, and another,

Until most of the jar had been emptied. *Finish the rest*,
Darrell's grandmother urged, solicitously, the green olives

Tasting like *abandon* and *freedom*. Their succulence
Complimenting a common lunch. Tonight, when I wake

I think of the green olives, flecked with red pepper flakes,
That I have in the refrigerator, and can nearly taste them,

Their lush pungence blossoming across my palate,
And think about the wild abandon of Gorky's street urchins

In *My Childhood*. I think about making a running break
Past the grazing cows along the hillocks of the slope

Of that verdant hill, and coming to know the taste
Of green olives and how they open out across the tongue,

Filling the mouth with the nascence of language,
That led me to feast on untold meals of freedom and song.

Flowering

For three days that April,
    we followed the trail
        up to a green meadow —

its deep color lush after
    the winter rains; and sitting
        among the California poppies,

that studded the grasses
    with an orange pointillism,
        a young blonde woman sat,

wearing nothing but
    hiking boots, her pack
        beside her, amid that flowering.

We stopped and spoke
    in a casual demeanor, but
        as in the myth of the divine

feminine, in which she
    challenged the male gods,
        who had just happened upon

her, in moving
    the feather she had placed
        in the air between them, and,

no matter how
    hard they blew their
        breath, they were powerless

in their being able
    to even touch it,
        there was a similar element

of the unmovable
    among each of us,
        an aspect of gravity that kept

us apart, but
    brought us together
        by the magnetizing force

of the allure of her body,
    of that astonishment,
        as she sat, enthroned, on

the sloping hillside
    of orange poppies,
        sunbathing in her boots.

The Knowing

What has awakened you is not
So much the headlights of your

Neighbor's car illuminating the walls
Of the room at 2:00 a.m. as much

As the cold hard rain from the violent
Thunderstorm that probably destroyed

The flower heads of the purple
And yellow flags of the iris, unaware

Of their nobility, after only a day
They began blooming. The present

Moment is more of that, the knowing
Of that moment deeply, and then

Remembering what you saw on the face
Of your friend, how she acted like a deer

Ready to bolt across a meadow
She couldn't run fast enough to traverse

Because the malevolent actions
Of many who live in this world are

Too much to bear. The present moment
Remains. It is all we ever have, and in it,

We inherit everything, a container that
Holds all and nothing, always becoming,

Transforming itself into being from
This to something less and then

Something more; as the rain starts again,
Falling harder, the lightning flashing

Across the dark sky, yellow streaks
Flaring in the purple petals of the iris.

Daylilies

When I left this morning,
    under a deep cerulean sky,
        the orange daylilies were thronging

the mailbox beside
    the road, petals still
        closed, beaded with droplets of dew;

so much green in the grass, in the trees,
    the sunlight streaking everything,
        making all sparkle, infusing every color

with shades of gold and yellow.
    When I returned just before noon,
        the daylilies had opened their supple

orange mouths,
    tasting the air, savoring the breeze
        with tongues of anther and pistil;

the chiffon of their
    throats offered the coolness
        of song and practical shade and nectar

for a pollinating bee.
    They hold as much
        gladness as we can imagine, filling us

with orange rapture,
    the orange of daylilies,
        rising on stems by the roadside farm;

the lithe cups of their mouths,
    spilling over with urgency,
        with exultation, unfolded and full,

blooming with heedless
    abandon, with pleasures
        so tantalizing they invite us to look,

to breathe the diligence
    of their color, to be as bedazzled
        as they at the pinnacle of their lives.

A Way of Seeing

When I saw the first
    monarch of mid-summer,
        so transfixed was I by its dark orange wings,

I hesitated for what may
    have been an eternal instant, when
        I said aloud, *Monarch*, and it flew around me,

as it might around a milkweed
    pod, although the milkweed has
        not quite ripened here in mid-July. It floated

around me like a friend,
    an ally; it settled on the ground, to display its
        wings, fanning them open, fanning them closed,

then leaving them unfolded,
    to reveal the small finger-length of black
        thorax and abdomen, the white spots bejeweling

the black rims of its wings
    that divide the lush orange,
        as if they were panes of stained glass, fanned

and fanned again,
    as if to say, *How well made; how*
        orange my wings that migrate south thousands of miles;

or maybe I spoke
    those words aloud, no matter;
        because, when I moved, the monarch rose up,

and sauntered across
    summer air. I stopped, breathed in
        a reminder of the morning, a brightness and

fulfillment vanishing;
    endangered and soon extinct, as
        when we look and see, there in the empty air.

Summer Rain

Its patter is distinguished, its rhythm
Pools then pools within itself again.

It is the slow, persistent music of lovers
Who are at one in making their gazing

At God last long after their lovemaking
Is over. Just by the look on their faces,

The divine afterglow of their union
Is deepened by the mesmerizing

And seductive healing of the slow-falling
Nature of its meditative tympani.

It is the Paris of weather phenomena.
Who wouldn't imagine themselves

In the arms of their soul mate just by
The softness and rustle of its sound?

It is the freshness of the newly opened
Flowers of iris and peony nodding

To the beat in the coolness of its
Falling, sometimes a petal loosening

And dropping into a puddle in
The garden that is alive with its wetness.

Bouquet

There are layers of loveliness
to all of this —

this is what the many-petaled
roses know —

imagine that fragrance,
the unfurling

of that which is within their
petals in their opening

to the world; but then again
the fragrance of that is what

this is, which also fills us
with the sweet abundance

in ourselves, as
we open and reopen with

the distillation of that
bouquet further clarifying

each other, as if
we were spiraling upward

toward the light, through
the lattice work of a trellis,

or reaching through
the mirrors reflecting us,

as fluid as water,
for each other's hands.

Mint

Mist rises from the ridge
    of Long Mountain after the thunderous
        morning rains. By noon the heat has swept

away the coolness lavished
    by the storms. Walking beside the thicket,
        the fragrance of mint permeates the air with

such a deep pungence of herbal
    earth that its rich odor could be a color,
        such as yellow, and that its perfume is of such

an effect that it possesses
    a brightness that becomes enflamed
        in the rising heat of the day. That the mint

had been cut back to provide
    a view of the traffic passing on the road,
        it is similar to what forgiveness may be, in that

after mint is cut its fragrance
    suffuses the very air we breathe;
        that the smell might adhere to our clothes,

and certainly instills the redolence
    of it in our memory, is specific
        to the act of the mint being sheared, or what

act initiated the necessity
    of forgiveness, which then lead to the balm
        that we may think of being a comforting tea.

Only if we were more
	akin to mint itself could we
		release such an essence, and so immediately;

although the mint could prove
	to us a salient lesson, one
		that would be easy to remember, to attest by,

if by any slander, or insult,
	even great offense, that has cut us,
		to recall how the oils of mint are released

when their stems are rendered, and what
	richness in healing pervades the nostrils of
		all those who are fortunate to just inhale.

The Snail

It isn't in reaching the crest
    of the rise of the gorge
        and already wading in the sound

of the rush of the brook.
    Nor is it in standing above
        the flume just before the waterfall

and watching the lacy
    stream flow over its bed,
        flecked with white quartz below

its ripples. Neither
    is it in pausing
        to watch the snake pour its ribbons

over the dirt and
    the stones on the path.
        All of that gives its own reason for

awakening within,
    with a plentitude
        of spirit, but it is in seeing the snail

in a streak of sunlight
    falling in a band across
        the trail, in a plank of light. It is in

seeing this snail's spiral
    mollusk shell, its pink Lilliputian
        face and black-tipped horns rising

to meet your face as
 you look down toward its
  glistening body, lavished in its own

viscosity, in the dew,
 in the golden light of the sun.
  It is this miracle that you will carry

with you as does
 the snail its earth house shell
  wherever you will go, always

remembering the spiral
 emblem leading within
  itself and out of itself in such

a fluid and harmonic
 fashion, whose circular
  design is an image of the divine.

The Treadle and the Light

The spirit is the treadle, often with a foot to the floor
Making up for lost time. The soul is the memory

Of the last time you saw your mother happy, while
Picnicking with you and a friend of hers

From New Jersey, on a beach in Miami, two weeks
Before she died after walking you to school

On the first day of third grade, only a week after
Having arrived with your father in a move north

To New England, where she thought you would have
A better life. The soul is what you have seen

In the face of your lover. It is the light that floods out
Of the face of the one woman you have loved

In your life, whose radiance fills you, then fills you
Again, and in whom you find what is oceanic.

It is what you discover in the brimming and singing,
And the singing and brimming in that. The spirit is

The feeling of the push and pull of our oars
In the water; how the strokes of our favorite pen

Sound, scratching across a sheet of paper; the cut
Crystal that holds that one glass of bistro wine that

You savor after dinner. The soul is more renown,
Since we seem to hear more talk about it,

But the more we talk about it, the less it appears.
It is the cartographer, who is an exile, in the vastness

Of a country without a name. The soul enjoys
Sleeping in; although if you reach for it in the middle

Of the night, you'll discover that it has risen early
To take a walk, or to go fishing, or to just pace,

With its boots thudding on the porch, in deciding
Upon which one to do, or both, or neither.

The spirit wants to have finally made a selection
Of which diamond sparkling in the case is the one

To choose. But the soul, when it is time to turn
Around, and to access the presence in order to look

Into the perpetuity in your lover's eyes, is the Puccini
In our lives. It is the *Nessun Dorma* playing without

A tenor and an orchestra. Although it is the music
Of the vision, it is also the vision of the music.

The Victrola on the Label

Mrs. Kevetchan and my grandmother would bask
Together, each in her own chaise lounge,

In the afternoons in Miami in the 1950s,
And sip iced drinks through a straw from

Pastel-colored aluminum or plastic containers.
They would do so sometimes after a morning

In the kitchen making dozens of pierogies,
Consisting of potato or prune fillings, that would

Be followed by their having lunch, which
Would often include boiled chicken

Or *golumpki*, cabbage leaves rolled with ground
Beef. There beneath the mango tree

They would revel in the intoxicating Floridian
Sunshine, each in their housecoats with faded

Tulips and daffodils, that alerted me
To their sadness regarding their deceased husbands.

They would languish together reminiscing about
How lucky they were to leave Eastern Europe

Before Hitler's tanks motored over the Polish cavalry;
Before Warsaw was cordoned off and made into

A ghetto of death; before the black smoke rose
Into the wound that was cut into the sky

From the smokestacks in the camps of barbed wire.
They would recall the days working at RCA,

In New Jersey, where they reminded me
That is where the records were manufactured,

With the image of a little dog cocking her head
Towards the Victrola on the label, as if

To hear the music better. As a child, I imagined
What music the little dog might be listening to,

And it wouldn't be until I was in my late teens
That I would read Chekhov's *Lady with Lapdog*;

Although what lit up my child's mind
With tantalizing delight was Mrs. Kevetchan

Asking me if I wanted to see her *little doggie*,
To which I would display my avid pleasure;

And how she would reach for her purse,
Then open it, and lift up her toy Chihuahua,

Whose miniscule body would tremble and shake
On his miniature legs, his bulging eyes shining.

Only to return him to the large pocketbook
Next to her lounge chair, where she assured me

The dog would be kept safe and cool. Whenever
I recall Mrs. Kevetchan and her little dog,

I think about the wonder of her life, that she
Savored afternoons beneath a mango tree

In a land Ponce de Leon discovered in his search
For *The Fountain of Youth*, for her to have outlived

A job in a factory to afford to retire, and not only
Purchase a pocketbook to outdo all handbags, but

Also to buy a dog small enough to fit inside of it
And to bring it with her wherever she would go.

Sooey

The time the drove escaped from their pen from the farm
across the road, they moved in a huddle over the lawn,

red-cheeked and pink in their muddied nakedness, cheery
in their sanguine abandon, snorting in their anticipation

of their approaching the compost pile beside the barn.
They jiggled when they moved, ears cocked,

ruddy-faced, in their collective charge forward together,
insouciant in their newfound freedom, just the oh, yes

of them a pleasure to observe in their open delight that
was as sheer of a thing as they were of a weighty heft.

Gregarious in their gait together in their small herd, they
launched themselves forward with an intelligence that

seemed to be fertile in their brains, more so, than other
animals, apparently protective of each other as they were

of themselves, seemingly motivated in that they bore
resemblance more to humans, especially in the glib look

on their faces, and that they moved about in the world
not so much at random but that they had intent, a plan

that included one for all and all for one, in their reaching
the kale stems, apple cores, and still-juicy melon rinds

that they so auspiciously found among coffee grounds
in the compost, before their farmer, smiling broadly,

brought them back to the sparseness of their
wooden pens, spattered with a wealth of mud, as tines

of the farmer's pitchfork tickled them from behind,
the lilt of his chanting call of sooey the alchemical charm

to bring them home, snouts turned upwards, mouths
open, congenially returning, squeaking nasal oinks,

throaty and full, on the run; the beauty in them, seeing
them come; the joy about them, in seeing them go.

Quintessence

Dawn quiet, late August,
on Market Hill Road, and I am finishing

moving into the Robert Francis cottage
that I will forever refer to as a cabin;

and I see them: spotted doe and fawn
walking the road's sandy edge;

and they are so nonchalant about
my sighting them and their seeing me

that I could be one of them.
But it was the fawn's antics that made my

seeing them memorable, with her springing
into the air beside the doe;

the doe observing with approval, the fawn
stepping a few feet, then rising

straight up in the air, front legs tucked,
the back legs fully extended —

becoming all of what it was supposed to be,
and emblematic of itself —

absolute and iconic in that pose;
and indelibly etched in a moment of time,

its energizing spirit cresting through
late summer mist, the chill in the air

emanating more from the naked bounce
of its enthusiasm, portending for me

the grace of the years of living in those
woods; herald who presaged such things

by its vaulting in mid-air with such sheer
delight that it endures as not only an image

within me but also abides as a constant
in the instant of what it inspires —

of what it is to be alive, of embodying
the quintessence of leaping and bounding.

Ode to End of Summer

Sunlight flickers over the lushness of August,
fills even the slender inflorescence

of stalks of timothy, as a flock
of cedar waxwings flies in and out of the hedge

of honeysuckle. Luxuriant halcyon weather
will give way to the flurry and the early chill

of September busyness not dissimilar to the way
the windy poplar lets go of its leaves in such

a burst and with such flare; and letting go
is what we need to do. What a delight to have

leftover morsels of lobster marinating in butter
from last night's dinner, that I serve over

four toast points, spread with mayonnaise
and paprika; accompanied with a salad

of garden fresh tomatoes, snow peas,
shredded carrot, and sweet onion in olive oil

and balsamic, tossed with julienned basil leaves,
cracked black pepper, and Kosher salt.

I finish the plate with a garnish of two grape
leaves stuffed with spearmint and rice.

To celebrate the relinquishing of summer
only makes room for more appreciation

of what was savored and the harvest to come.
To ready ourselves for the harvest we offer

our gratitude to every bite of shellfish and
the medley of vegetables that

they will nourish us and might place us in
balance with the windy poplar releasing

its flurry of leaves and what may be nature's
harmonic asymmetry, igniting us into verb.

Dinner with Camus

I plate both halves of the omelette, one half for now,
one for later; and hear his voice: debonair, erudite,

sweetly gruff, *Merci beaucoup*, he says; and takes a plate,
then sits opposite me. Switching to English, he asks,

*Why did you put in garlic with the sautéed sweet potatoes
and onions.* I tell him, *It is because I love a woman, and that*

*she loves me, but now we only see each other when I visit her
at her office.* Camus answers that Sartre and de Beauvoir

lived separately. He adds, *It was unconventional; however,
their love perpetuated itself. It lasted; it wasn't a convenience*

that they celebrated, but each other. I ask him, *Did they fight?*
He answers with his eyes, lifts a forkful of omelette into

his mouth, then says, *Since we all argue about life itself, then
why shouldn't lovers argue about love, even if they do so silently.*

Before I can ask another question, he queries me about
why I added the sweet bell peppers and the sun-dried

tomatoes to the omelette, and I reply, *Because I wanted
to sing. I wanted to recollect what was fine about last summer;*

*making dinner for Julieanne. Since I had frozen the peppers,
I wanted to eat them before the fine weather this summer.*

He stares quizzically, but compassionately, then asks,
Why? I push my plate aside, surprised to finish

before him, since I am such a slow eater, then answer,
Because I am passionate about the simple mathematics of the lyric.

He reaches over to help himself to another glass of wine,
and says, *It is exquisite for me just to taste this again, holding*

the bottle of Baron d'Arignac up to the light fading
through the two windows beside the table. *Just like*

Meursault when he makes an omelette after his mother dies,
and has a glass of wine with it, in L'Etranger, I ask, knowing

the scene by heart. *Oui*, he responds, and looks out
into the falling dusk. *Did Meursault fire the extra shots*

into the Algerian, thinking it didn't matter, since he was dead
already? I ask him, nearly feeling a little heady from

a second glass of wine. *It didn't matter at that point, but*
everything matters all the time; what mattered was Meursault's

freedom, unenviable as his decision may have been, he explains.
I want to respond that I follow him, but since I don't,

I say, *Then what about Meursault's sense of freedom*
after he is tried and condemned to death? He eases back

his chair, then replies, *You are a commendable cook,*
and I am appreciative that you know my work so well.

Alerted to his imminent departure, I ask, *Must you leave*
so soon? He responds, *We all must go, unfortunately.*

The Lawrence Durrell *Alexandria Quartet* Mediterranean Cold Plate Dinner Special

The Justine: A pound of chilled broiled salmon,
Marinated in butter and lemon juice.
The Balthazar: Six ears of sweet corn,
Shaved off the cob; one small red onion,

Minced in large pieces, peasant-style;
One can of small white pinto beans; sufficient
Amounts of olive oil and balsamic vinegar; one
Teaspoon of chili powder; mix ingredients; chill.

The Mount Olive: Half a pound of green beans,
Seared *al dente* (medium heat; two to three
Minutes) in olive oil; golden raisins;
Dried sliced apricots, a handful of walnuts;

Abundant chunks of crumbled feta, toss
With a splash or two more of olive oil; chill.
The Clea: One large zucchini, halved, then
Quartered at an angle; seared *al dente* (medium

Heat; three to five minutes, on the flat side);
Allow to cool. (Recommendation:
Drizzle some of the oil from the skillet
Onto the salmon when plating the meal.)

Arrange all of the above, lyrically,
Onto plates, so that each may begin to speak
The truth, in their turn. Suggested beverage:
Iced coffee, with crushed ice and cream,

Or half and half. Alternate beverage
Suggestions for those gentle reprobates
With an interest in a taste of debauchery:
Chilled Spanish Cava *or* Vin de Cassis

(Any chilled inexpensive, dry French white
Wine mixed with no more than a drop or two
Of Creme de Cassis). Serves: Four. Restores
The body and the mind and reinvigorates

The spirit, like the mild but steady wind
Off the ocean at dusk — pungent with that
Piquant kiss of salt in the air that seasons
Each of us to the depth of our very soul.

Nautilus Shell

You have become
old; every winter the cold cuts deeper into your bones.

You have become this
matrix of presence connected to memories —

that biology kit, as Christmas gift,
when you were twelve, that snowless holiday in 1965 —

to that lifetime ago
when you were a young man,

the one whose dreams and losses you have eclipsed —
to now, toward the end,

as you hold the hollowness of all that
like an empty nautilus shell, whose spiral mollusk shape

holds everything and nothing, whose resonance within
issues with the sounds of the sea,

in the crashing of waves —
along the coast of a familiar, but otherworldly, shore.

Etched

We dispel the notion
that poems can be tossed off,

that there are tricks
to jump-starting their success,

that there are any number
of ways to achieve

lasting resonance
within them. We portend

that poetry is written
with similar intent

as the lines that are etched
across the palms of our hands.

from

Things I Know I Love:
Odes to Food

(2015)

Blue Chicory

Its petals may be described as vivid blue,
but if anything they are the color of the silence

of an early morning summer sky. Unlobed
and pointed leaves spread along its rough,

grooved stem by any roadside. Its nicknames
include *succory* and *coffeeweed*, but my favorite

is *ragged sailor*. In Puglian cuisine, the leaves
of wild chicory are mixed with fava bean puree,

known as *Fave e Cicorie Selatviche*. Wild chicory
leaves are bitter, but their bitterness can be

reduced if the leaves are boiled. It is also
suggested that they are then sautéed with garlic,

and combined with pasta. The root
was ground and adopted as a coffee substitute

by soldiers during the Civil War. *Puntarelle*,
a common meal in Rome, is made with

chicory sprouts. Due to their protein
and fat content, chicory roots have been used

as a desired alternative for horses. According
to European folklore, chicory is also believed

to unlock doors. Although it may be best known
when it is cultivated as radicchio, sugarloaf,

or Belgian endive. After all, Horace wrote:
As for me, olives, endives, and mallows provide.

Let me set my table by chicory's providence,
and lay my dishes out to await its many gifts,

as the shadows of birds pass over my setting
of silverware and plates to disappear

across the sky that, if anything, only
resembles the vivid blue of chicory petals.

The Dante Alighieri Summer *Paradiso Al Fresco*

It is not yet your vacation, but it could be —
The day being so perfectly lit beneath

The high cerulean sky, dotted with cumulus;
The air so fresh after days of June rain.

You decide to take out the leftover spinach
Pasta and white clam sauce from the refrigerator;

Dust it generously with *Parmesan-Romano-Asiago*,
Rotate several full turns of black pepper

From the wooden grinder, and drizzle a couple
Of tablespoons of virgin olive oil over all of that.

You have worked your way through all the levels
Of hell: your irascible boss, the impossible job.

And then persevered through all seven
Of the purgatorial circles, much described

By that beloved flirt, Saint Theresa of Avila,
Who it is said levitated several times in the galley

Kitchen of the nunnery to the extent that
Her fellow sisters needed to pull her by her habit

Back down to the ground. By now you can use
A respite in paradise, although a half hour would

Do; besides, where you find yourself now
Appears to be the Florian, a sidewalk café, with

The most fascinating of angelic faces at each table.
In your abandon, you order the side salad to go

With the pasta, which is simply called the *Al Fresco*,
Combining chick peas, cucumber, and Vidalia onion

In Tahini dressing. When the waitress
Takes your order, you don't notice the size

Of her wings until she turns to go; and before
You can speak the thought, she turns back around

And suggests a drink that she believes best to
Accompany your meal. As you take another sip

Of the iced cherry juice with orange seltzer,
You notice the trio sitting at the table next to you.

Proffering his violin as the sacred object that it is,
Is Vivaldi; then beside him, Dante is sharing

Photographs of himself and Beatrice, taken
On their vacation in the Pyrenees, to Botticelli,

Who is sitting in front of a plate full of empty
Shells from his abundant appetizer of clams casino —

All three originals beaming in the verisimilitude
Of their specific and inimitable perfections,

All seated beneath a sword of light the Archangel
Gabriel is holding above them like a torch of flame.

Things I Know I Love

First, it was seeing the fresh sweet corn
　　placed in rows of high stacks around
　　　　the stand that a South Amherst neighbor keeps on

her front lawn; and this then led
　　to my thinking about the one celebratory
　　　　meal I savor every summer, which is mussels and

sweet corn salad. So, I selected
　　a half dozen ears of corn, and brought
　　　　them home, to which I added certain ingredients

to, after I boiled the ears: white pinto
　　beans; sweet onion; freshly squeezed
　　　　lemon; chili powder, to which I drizzled a mixture

of olive oil and balsamic over
　　the fresh mussels that I added —
　　　　the poor man's, or the everyman's, fruit of the sea.

What punctuated my concluding
　　the preparation of the salad, which I
　　　　placed into the refrigerator to chill, that I will savor

for several dinners, with
　　a glass of an affordable Bordeaux, was
　　　　my listening to Mozart's *Linz Symphony*. The music,

is one of lavish
　　abandon and of proclamation.
　　　　If Mozart loved anything, and he loved many things;

he loved his wife,
     Constanze; and he had a fancy for expensive
          shoes, as I might love summer and my celebrating it

by listening to
     his composition, which Mozart
          dedicated to the citizens of Linz; and after being

bathed in my own joy
     I have created what is
          symphonic, in a gustatory and culinary tribute to

summer, with a salad
     of delectable mussels
          and dewy-eared sweet corn, to share with friends.

Ray's Sandwich Shop

Some walk-in closets were larger.
Ray and his wife laid the prepared sandwiches

across the blue Formica counter.
Bologna, salami and provolone, ham salad

on wheat or white —
and the real charm of having them all wrapped

in waxed paper,
with the prices marked with a sharpie: 95 cents

to $1.95, which was how much my favorite
cost, tuna salad with Swiss. Add a bag of chips

and an orange soda, and lunch was under $3.00.
Winter days they would have homemade chili

or chicken noodle soup steaming in a vat
on a large hot plate. Every morning they had

coffee, light and sweet; tea with lemon; fresh
pastries: New York-style, both cheese and fruit.

They were always aproned and busy —
the windows often steamed with bodies pressed

close. They were not only short, but
they were small, and Ray would flip up the end

of the counter,
dash to the cooler through the waiting crowd;

dart back again, fill another order, make change;
and he would flash that broad Phil Silvers grin.

They put their daughters through college
and fed a generation of students and the faculty,

filing in and out in their pea coats and tweeds.
Two thirds of my life gone past,

but I remember often standing beside Sigourney
Weaver, who would have walked across

the street from the Art & Architecture building,
where she would be among the tallest

in line, attired in her black leather jacket;
and, on occasion, Meryl Streep, as luminous as

a Botticelli, blonde
tresses flying, having just stepped offstage from

rehearsal at
the Rep, directly opposite Ray's Sandwich shop.

The Autumnal

It begins by cherishing the moment
I think I will always have of those

leaves of the luminous maple bordering
the Quabbin Reservoir Gate 31

parking lot lit in my mind. I have never
quite seen as brilliant and infused

an orange as that — nearly another crisp
shade all unto its own design.

Although it leads to not wanting to
relinquish the remaining chili seeds

at the bottom of the olive container,
which I pour a beaten egg into,

and whisk so as to blend in the red and
yellow flecks, resembling the autumnal

leaves of the maple ablaze in its colors.
Then I create a small omelette from this

by adding slices of avocado and Swiss,
after placing the egg mixture into

a skillet where I had browned leftover
red potatoes with sweet Inca onions.

When I serve this with a buttered
English muffin, with Morello cherry

preserve, orange juice, and fresh-perked
coffee, it is not only just nourishment

that I ingest but also further learn to
savor the present moment of my life,

which often opens to include shades
that are nearly as crisp unto their own

designs, and where leaf fall itself is
its own harbinger of both imminent

decay and eminent crown of what has
been and what is bound to come —

of what it is that shines through
in its myriad ways, infused with light

and the inimitable and inevitable
falling through the flurry of its falling.

from

Candling the Eggs

(2017)

Silhouette

Due to the density of the falling snow, I can barely see her
perched in the crown of a tree I am not able to identify,

just standing on the cusp of the pasture across the road.
The snow acts as a veil, one that is not rippling, but

streaming, so white, it is nearly blinding to the eyes —
even appearing as mist, but moving more horizontally than

vertically; mist blowing in on itself, falling and not rising.
As I approach the roadside from the farmhouse, I can see her

better, but because of the rush of the snowfall, which resembles
a divine white madness released from the sky, which I hear

wetly striking random flakes before they accumulate among
themselves on the ground. Her visage is darkly spectacular —

what I gauge to be nearly two feet high, standing tall on
a broken branch atop the tree, creating her own shadowy *noir*.

Until I take one too many slow steps forward, and the red-
tail can bear no further intrusion, since it is her tree and her

meadow, her sky and her own world, she rises up on the broad
span of her wings, and disappears into a seam of the snowstorm,

with apparent exclamation, as if she might be saying:
I have watched you closely, for some time, but you are one

of them, and it is your kind, as I have observed, from my aerie,
that have ruined the earth.

What Is Essential

You've gone to the finest school, Miss Lonely
But you know you only used to get juiced in it
Bob Dylan, "Like a Rolling Stone"

What the checkout clerk said burned with a new ridiculousness,
a pervasive absurdity, another torque of snarkiness,

in joking to an associate — they are no longer called colleagues —
about calling in sick *while you were in the building*, which buzzed

with a crackle of neon that lit up the pool in the parking lot
beneath it that was yellow with vomit then blue with rain,

that represented what was repelling about the malignancy
that entitlement is in America —

that false sense of reality at the corrupt core of the country
and the malaise of college students who protest because

they believe they have every right to get drunk and destroy
private property in a public demonstration —

crushing beer cans on other people's lawns in the spring mud
instead of marching against war,

hunger, the new fascism in politics, bullying in the workplace,
the sickness in the very character of what is contemporary.

The Female Cardinal

Watching the birds this morning use the budding
adolescent maple as a stage from which they

dive to the ground and then rise up again, I see
the blue jay, with all of his braggadocio, flutter

and fluster on the branches, and poke his beak
among the leaf litter, then leave; a mourning dove,

in all of its natural coyness, coo and peck, then
alight upon the driveway's crushed black basalt

where it selects flecks of grain no other bird seems
to be able to find; but then a female cardinal

begins her flight-dance among the maple's limbs,
charming in her practical but fashionable colors —

wearing her rouge liming just the edges
of her wings and highlighting the top of her head;

with just enough mascara to accentuate
the sparkle of her eyes; her beak sun-colored with

an element of gold; her feathers not the bright red
of her male counterpart, but she wouldn't have it

otherwise, since she blends her feathers within
her environment with their rich shades of beige

and brown. There she is not missing a windblown
seed among last autumn's mottled leaves, adept

and confident, obviously feeling quite smart
in her avian regalia, apparently not out to beat up

on the boys, and to sing about it later, since
that is not her way, but yielding to the female

principle inherent within her as she gives way to
the puddles in the culvert by hopping around them.

She gains strength in herself by not trying to be
what she is not, and discovering the deep parity

in that, as she answers the whistle of her mate,
the delight evident in her tone, and as cardinals

do, whistles her response back, as if to say, *I'm
over here. What else is new? And what about you?*

The Leper

So, this is what it feels like,
　　this longing to begin again,
　　　　this urge thriving to be alive, to be in

a new body, of having another
　　start, to reconsider what it is
　　　　to be conscious, to launch into living

with urgency, of finding the verve
　　of the moment in every moment
　　　　this spring day, the dogwood beginning

to blossom, the maples budding
　　red, farm fields furrowed open again.
　　　　Then there is also the loathing of those

who have systematically exiled you,
　　and you who are also helplessly
　　　　part of that process. That needs to be

realized. Those who ascribe
　　to any spiritual practice would
　　　　proselytize that it needs to be exorcised —

the hate of those who
　　have injured you, and those who
　　　　persist in injuring you, is so vital that it is

imperative to own that first before
　　there is any possibility of letting it go.
　　　　The enormity of it, and its burning, that

consumes you, becomes a force
    of its own, that necessitates
        a new growth ring in the bole of the tree.

So the rejuvenation in spring is a part
    of that, of dealing with the bliss of renewal,
        in conjunction with all that is impaired

and wildly sprung from
    suppurating wounds, slow to heal, that
        smolder in the soul. Exiles are forced

to abandon communities
    they were outcast from; may
        I become a leper in my enclave of one,

might the bells I wear fend you off,
    as I heal myself in the solitude that
        I embrace; may I abandon my antipathy

of all those who have exiled me
    in exercising their own fears of making peace
        with the outcast leper in each of themselves.

Candling the Eggs

It was the candled egg that I remember
  that Mrs. Dornisch held up to the flame,
    and its total eclipse against the darkness

of the damp cellar of her farmhouse,
  the air heavy with the odor of the hens,
    that floated as feathers do in the air.

Always feel safe here, she said to me,
  and I always did, with her by my side,
    her aproned warmth distinguished by

the cookies she might have stuffed into
  one of the pockets, her momentary
    musing uttered in *sotto voce*, which

deepened the privacy of our candling
  the eggs, the condensation on the cellar
    walls evoking what my mother told me

in a story about what the catacombs
  looked like, so that the time I spent in
    Mrs. Dornisch's cellar with her became

what was one of my first spiritual
  experiences, the quiet there so superb
    that I recall whenever I had a thought,

no matter how small it was, that
  Mrs. Dornisch could hear it. The quiet
    and the candlelight amid the darkness

softening the harshness
       of my father's wrathful temper when
              my mother would walk me over there,

next door, during the times
       his rage breached what she might
              have thought to be some level of reason.

My father who never missed a day
       at the factory, but who could only speak
              broken English, was ridiculed at work,

then vent verbal fury
       at the injustices; while Mrs. Dornisch,
              a septuagenarian, and myself, perhaps

aged three, candled the eggs, as two
       anchorites might have applied gilt to
              the letters in an illuminated manuscript,

bound in vellum; and as our breaths
       steamed in the coolness of the cellar,
              one at a time, the eggs would be added

to the coiled metal basket, clicking against
       the tops of some of the others, as a golden
              halo flickered in the hallowed darkness.

Milk Snake

Your colors blend
　　with dirt and flecked leaf litter,
　　　　your patterned loops marked

beside the warm
　　bricks of the porch steps
　　　　where we found you at noon

in full sun;
　　the tact of
　　　　your name, taken from legend —

where you sucked
　　the udders of pastured cows;
　　　　and your nickname *farmer's friend,*

ridding barn and field
　　of insects to benefit a stout
　　　　crop. Today when I watch, you

bask in your warm spot,
　　your full arm's length
　　　　only three-quarters in view, tail

still under
　　the last layer of
　　　　siding. I step a touch too near;

you reel in flesh
　　and scales, a jack-in-a-box
　　　　who rids our home of rodents,

met in the vise-
    grips of jaws
        and your body's sinewy muscles.

Tonight when I flick
    on the porch light,
        you will slide away in a fluid S

from beneath
    my shadow, sweeping your
        length over a crackle of leaves.

Imminence

in memory of Jerzy Kosinksi

It had rained or it was about to rain,
as you stood in the threshold of the doorway
of the bookstore, a small entourage

surrounding you. I remember a woman taller
than you, a fur wrap around her shoulders;
and others, a man in a trench coat with

salt and pepper hair. You looked powerful
but tentative, at once. I recognized
the darkness in your face from the pages

of *The Painted Bird*, which I had devoured,
aghast by the tale of your survival; then
read again, exhilarated as I might have

taken the same roller coaster ride,
by it having frightened me even more than
it did the first time, just for the sake of

the thrill of being alive. You looked up at
us on the raised platform of the front desk
as you might be squinting into a light

that was brighter than it is comfortable
to see into, and I asked you
questions about your writing, how you

were, if I could help you find anything,
could you please come on in;
and what I saw there in your visage were

the atrocities that the war tattooed onto you,
although you did escape the humiliation
of the Nazis branding numbers on one

of your wrists. The child in you never fully
having escaped hanging from a ceiling lamp,
or a chandelier, while a German Sheppard

placed in the room with you, leapt and
snapped at whatever appendage hung low
enough when you tired; and the child

you were did not escape the shadows that
accompanied your fierce sense of freedom
while running through the forest because

all the shadows kept pace with you —
as fast as you could run, you could not outrun
the shadows and the accrued darkness

of what had occurred to you. Still, I was
shocked when I read, some years later, that
you had taken your own life, that it was

impossible for you to have outdistanced
the war and your memories of it,
that it haunted you, that it was imminent

in the gravity of the creases of the wrinkles
in your face that reminded me
it had stormed or it was about to storm.

The Wood

1   The first time I met Ted Esposito
his eyes were darkened within their sockets,

story was that a woman he had been involved
with had left him, and he bore the wound

visibly, the way grace is achieved through
the hard love of humility, in quietude.

He was a masseuse, who worked
in New York three days a week, and he was

dedicated to Zen, had a teacher
from the East, in a zendo in the city.

The progress Ted made in his practice
outdistanced all speculation, he began to walk

with an inner glow about him. His balance
was such that when you stood and spoke

with him, he embraced you with the harmony
that vibrated within him.

His roshi in the city was so jealous
of the level of the satori he attained that their

relationship suffered because of it.
Ted described his experience of meditation

as a circle, pointing to the wood of the front
counter of the bookstore, saying, *When you*

*begin, there is just the wood; and half-way
into it, you begin to see through the wood*

*itself; and then if you have the experience of
satori, the wood becomes the wood, again.*

2   The last time I saw Ted Esposito, it was
     standing at the walk light at the corner

     of Temple and Crown, that is the second
     windiest corner in New Haven — the first

     being a block up, at the corner of Temple
     and Chapel, as the winds channel

     unimpeded through the concrete tunnels,
     fashioned by the buildings along

     the streets, all the way down to the harbor,
     especially in winter. But now the pink

     and white dogwood were in bloom all over
     campus — true augurs of spring, lending

     definition to the concept of commencement.
     Ted suggested to me that Zen meditation

     may not be my own way to realize
     enlightenment; but, added, not unlike

     the breakthrough Whitman experienced,
     that a devotion to writing, just might

     be the way — and as I turned to answer him,
     he had vanished, disappearing as Han-Shan

     did on Cold Mountain, as I looked one way,
     then another — hearing only in the echo

     of his voice, a cosmic
     laughter bouncing off of the brownstones.

Ode to the Iris

The iris are blooming in the garden
    again with their unfurled flags
        of petals open to catch rainwater.

Your name means rainbow, after
    the Greek goddess, *Iridaceae*, mother
        of Eros, and counterpart to Hermes.

Their royal purple and lightning
    yellow inflect the beds with a stately
        natural elegance, giving the pages

in the daybook of our lives
    the vivid shades of their blossoming —
        a memory indicating refreshment

at the end of each May that is not
    to be taken for granted but to be
        revered, not so much to mark time's

passing but to remind us of presence.
    Each year the emerging of what is
        majestic about the iris is signaled by

violent thunderstorms, which don't
    seem to bother the peonies of June,
        already so drunk with themselves ants

run the petals of their sticky
    sweetness, as they collapse
        into the grass; whereas the iris stand

as sentries to the sovereign
        of what is resplendent, what is regal in
                us, what is supremely unconditional.

The noble iris always ready for each
        storm and its sheets of driving rain —
                never any complaint apparent in them

that they may have only opened
        for just an hour, or an afternoon,
                or a single day; and if their flower

heads should be shattered upon
        their long, elegant stems in the force
                of the downpour, although one may be

aware of its sisters about to burst
        their own pods, to bud among
                the blades of their leaves, is singularly

resolute in their being, swaying
        in sunlight and storm, as steadfast as
                their color, whose hues flower within us.

Reawakening

When I awoke this morning,
I asked for guidance: where was I supposed to be,

where should I go?
So, I made my pilgrimage to the Peace Pagoda,

and as I neared the pond,
each of my steps brushing through the grass,

muffled by the sound of
the wind, I stood atop a flat stone, where I noticed

Koi flashing through the water,
their bodies such a fulfilling shade of orange;

tadpoles darting among the roots of pond lilies;
the grass around me

thrumming with the buzz of bumblebees;
a bull frog beginning his mantra of *who-did-it*;

and draped unceremoniously
across a pointed rock protruding above the surface

of the water
was a sunning water snake; its length resting

in a series of serifs; banded
in bone-white circles spanning its circumference,

half the size of my wrist;
its head positioned in a hollow on the far side of

the outcrop.
Even as the prayer flags began to snap and ripple

on the stiff breeze, the stillness
of the snake remained still, coiled within itself;

and my stillness
stilled more within me; becoming nearly as still

as the snake's stillness; nothing bothering it, not
a thing disrupting me;

engaged in not being engaged —
its strength looped within itself, what was entwined

within itself basking
in a drowse on warm stone; powerful but inert —

all of more than three feet of it,
at peace in the world; and I at peace with it, having

become peaceful within myself.
Seeing through the water of the pond, observing

the glaze of sky on top of it, then the snake atop
the stone:

latent spine of kundalini, nascent bolt of shakti —
reawakening when it reawakens.

Dream Time

The time between snowmelt and first blooms,
after mud season and before even a hint
of new leaves; the mist hanging in the trees

as in dream time; the swirling fog so thick
it settled and opened, then resumed to form
before it lifted and vanished, with my having

the mountain to myself, three miles up
the wide main trail; the five hundred foot
vertical rise draped in oscillating white clouds;

the green masts of pine tops punctuating
the roiling mass; the quiet on the trail
so intensely pervasive that my breath steaming

the air registered its own pliant echo.
Although I was woodswalking in early spring,
I could have been entering *Purgatorio*,

without a guide. The woods became
not so much supernatural in the rising mist but
supremely earthy, the divine nearly revealing

itself within the commonplace of bark and rock
in the blowing fog. What did electrify a chill
up my spine was my sensing a presence

moving with my movements, not too distant
yet never that far away, stopping when I ceased
my own steps; but I discounted this perception

as the creation of my own imagination, until
I crested the last rise to the summit, and without
hesitation scaled the seven flights of the fire

tower to where I was completely occluded
in the whiteout of the brume; and then I heard it,
walking softly on all fours, stopping just beyond

the rim of burnt winter grass circling the metal
joists of the tower where the murk fumed.
Whatever it was took a turn around the tower,

then stopped briefly, before choosing to take
the steep trail down the mountain's north face,
as I stood atop the lookout in the blowing spume.

Interstices

I notice the small speckled black and white egg
on the red bricks of the walk.

Then my eyes move to the three prominent holes
beneath the azalea bush — linking

the one egg, smaller than a bird's, to its reptilian
mother. When I move the egg, shifting it with

the toe of my boot, I can see the tip is shattered,
and that three chips lay to its side, allowing a view

of its inhabitant inside. The shell's simple, rough
pattern is as practical as it is elegant:

its design is to become visually lost among colors
of the earth, to be indistinguishable from

the shade of the soil, flecked with white stones —
to even look like a stone itself, until

the snake's young cracks the shell to free itself
and to enter the garden of its life. Upon looking

inside, I see the stillbirth snug within its earth
house shape, coiled amidst itself, more snake

than embryo, but nevertheless not quite snake.
We mourn for many things, but perhaps what we

grieve the most for is what expires before it begins;
the nascent but malformed; what is insufficiently

finished and on the threshold of realizing its own
becoming. In apparently insignificant

ways and enormous ones, all through our lives,
we touch the interstices between

living and dying; amid solar light and lunar
emanation; among the rippling signature the wind

writes and its cursives that appear in the blowing
summer grasses; betwixt the cracked egg

of my positive intent and whether
your understanding of it moves freely in the world.

The Jar, the Rope, and the Snake

If a clay jar is only a clay jar
then the air it contains is the same

as all the air around and beyond it.
So, this is Atman; and can be

a meditation for anyone to find
Atman; and to continue to focus

on the Atman within oneself,
which with rigorous devotion

leads to the liberation from what is
a perpetual cycle of birth and death.

If a rope is not a snake and only
a rope, we may all breathe a sigh

of relief, since the rope as a rope,
or even the snake as a snake, are just

metaphorical examples of Maya; and
the rope remains wound in a circle,

whereas the snake eventually slithers
through the world only to wind its

length back into a circle again: rope
and snake being extensions of our ego.

If transcending both Maya and ego
is the arduous path to becoming aware

that we are not only Atman but are
also Brahmin, or the entire universe

itself, but without the illusion of it as
a city at night reflected in a mirror, then

we experience the bliss, like none other,
of seeing Brahmin in everything,

or as Shankara intimates, we begin to see
all of the animals limned by their auras.

Abhorrence

When a peaceful protest of the slaughter
of goats in India becomes violent when

local men riot and begin stoning women
protesters, leaving one woman in critical

condition, it is abhorrent. Whatever
the reason there would be any rationale

for endorsing the denigration of women
not only injures those subscribing to that

but also blinds those who chose to
throw stones and wounds their own inner

feminine. Denouncing women
and becoming so thoroughly engaged in

reviling them, is unacceptable
in whatever form, and only offers nettles

instead of salve to assuage the sting.
A solution to the issue could be

engendering a pedagogy in preventing
such a crime. The stoning of women

is unconditionally unacceptable,
and anyone who partakes in such an act,

among the rubble, does violence to
themselves, without their even knowing

they are doing so. If only they knew that
I art thou, they could possibly begin

to comprehend that it is
they themselves who are about to be

bludgeoned by the stones
in their hands, and that nothing except

atonement can absolve the rage
in their eyes, the blood beginning to

streak their own
faces, just as they take aim and throw.

Autumn: Ansonia, 1962

It was the autumn that Kennedy
visited the impoverished Housatonic Valley

and his motorcade drove through downtown
Ansonia, past the parochial school where two

of my buddies and I ran behind the president's
limousine, big-eyed, waving our small hands

in the air, until he turned around and offered us
the indelible memory of his inimitable

charm, in smiling and waving
back. It was the autumn my father took off

his black armband forever, after having worn
it for a year to honor my mother's death

the autumn before. He dated a woman from
the Polish neighborhood, and we once went to

the drive-in, where they both sat in the back seat
and left me in the front seat behind the wheel,

where I actually felt like the adult every time
my father's girlfriend said, *Are you sure*

you're alright, we wouldn't want you to go
cross-eyed looking at the film through

the spokes of the steering wheel, between
the long silences that buffered the mystery

of the pillowed darkness in the back seat.
Never once did I look back, but kept

my eyes on James Stewart and John Wayne
in *The Man Who Shot Liberty Valance*.

My father's girlfriend had won me
over, especially after we went to a Saturday

afternoon Wrestlemania, where she took me
to the ring before the matches so that

stars such as Bobo Brazil, whose specialty
was the *Coco Butt*; farm-fed Haystack Calhoun;

and menacing Killer Kowalski, the hero
of factory-working Poles, would sign autographs.

It was the autumn that I came to know the way
the cold moves in at twilight in New England —

how it settles within you with pervasiveness
that is tantamount to the falling of night,

with all of its stars flickering across the dome
of the sky. On such an evening, after I had

made various chemistry experiments
in large pots in my father's girlfriend's

kitchen, I played on the porch with a fellow
student from Saint Michael's, a blonde-haired

girl, named Veronica. How we moved
across the wide porch of the old Victorian

on a Connecticut mill town Saturday night.
It was if we danced, without touching,

our nine-year old hearts warmed by each other,
as our breaths smoked in the cold night air,

entranced by the magnetism of one another,
graced with the mysticism of not knowing why.

Heirloom

The heirloom roses have returned
on the cusp of May and June,

after having been over-pruned
two years before. First the pale green

leaves returned, with their deckled
and browned edges, as delicate as

handmade paper that holds hand set
type. Now, the tightly-furled rosettes

are appearing amid their foliage, as
if they might be shy of their beauty,

or even unsure of their lineage.
When the heirloom roses fully open,

I cut one or two from their rough
stems, lined with uneven rows of

thorns, and choose not to place them
in a vase, but float them in a bowl

of water, which I center
on the dining room table, so that

they can later be dried and stored
in a small, brown wicker basket,

with a cover, so that I might open it
sometime, months later, on occasion,

to remind me of the roses
and their petals that not only reside

in your heart but that also
enliven and are redolent in mine.

In Memory of Galway

Opening the door
this morning, I hear the

of gold-yellow oaks a
of the door beaded ·

remnants of wha
in your passing.

the trail of whic
that we brush
of which
sleeves
on
s

Nearly forty years ago, I remɛ..
table of a Chinese restaurant, named .

in New Haven, with myself and others for a poetr y
you were to give, and as it came to my turn to request

a poem that you might read later that spring evening —
the trees dropping blossoms across the sidewalks along

Linden Street — I asked for "The River that Is East,"
the one you wrote that regards Hart Crane.

You read that poem, among others, that evening,
the all-so-familiar shock of hair falling onto your forehead

that you would push back with the fingers of one hand,
to the delight of your audience,

Galway, always handsome as your poems were perennially
sturdy with their resonant humanity.

The question now remains is
that how can the fires of your loss staunch

the ensuing darkness other than
the words you bequeathed to us and that burn within us —

ch is laced with drops of melt
on the branches of the winterberry tree,

we shake from our dampened
reminding us of just how a branch snaps back

a sunny afternoon after heavy
now, leaving a whitened ghost hovering in the air, or

when we bend down to
notice a single glove lost by someone hurrying through

the storm, and recognize our own losses,
those ragged flags that blow as do the curtains drawn

out in the gale through the open windows of the heart,
alerting us to the lightning flash

of our very being that also
marks your death, not dissembling into the incorporeal,

beyond the gold-yellow and crimson trees
and that white line the horizon holds, then relinquishes.

Deer, in Three Movements

1   They gathered
on the far side of the brook after
my yellow Labrador made the turn
to gather the stick I had thrown
into the plunge pool, using her tail,
as a rudder, to stop, turn, and start
back to where I stood; and
I looked up to see the three does,
white tails flicking, studying me;
fervently twitching their black noses,
to discern whether I was enemy,
or friend, and before Cider could
make it back to the brook's bank,
shake herself, and drop the stick
for another possible round of fetch,
the three of them huffed, audibly,
their breaths clouding the air,
straightening themselves, having
seen enough, now disinterested,
their hooves beginning to echo
over the round stones protruding
from the mud of the far bank,
moving away in time to
that deep *tock, clop, tock, clop,*
I can still hear across the shale
and puddingstone shelf lining
the brook's banks, to merge into
a seam of the blowing mist rolling
across the greening acres
of meadow that is Haskins' Flats.

2   Whatever it might be
that just happens to go crashing
through thick woods always
sounds as if it is larger than
it is as it emerges into the open.
So, when I stopped hiking

and I came upon the scrub
meadow at the foot
of Mount Toby that overlooks
Cranberry Pond, due to those
sounds coming from the birch
grove, whose leaves flutter there,
my pounding heart and myself
expecting bear; the two of them
stumbled out of the woods
and came to a skidding halt,
entwined, as if their game of tag,
or whatever deer game they
were playing resulted in a tie,
since they were both *it*,
simultaneously. If deer can
look chagrined, these two
adolescents were taken aback
by their own ardor, as they
stared at me, an intruder now
made privy to their own sport,
their private frivolity, their
inimitable rites of becoming and
being deer. Whereas, I smiled,
and as they untangled hoof
and limb, they kept their eyes
on me, trusting me, perhaps,
only just a little bit, or maybe
hoping to, when they began
sauntering quietly back toward
the grove of windy birches,
looking all the more nonchalant,
turning their heads once before
soundlessly moving back again
among the boughs of summer.

3   Always in a rush,
this morning was no exception —

except there it was,
a buck, antlered, standing still
in the corner of the patch of land
I had cleared a year earlier
at the northeastern corner
of the knoll that is Fort Juniper,
on the side of the house
Robert Francis had the small
shed built, and where he would
sunbathe, in the privacy of leafy
trees, shielding him from the road.
Book bag over one shoulder,
coffee mug in one hand, car keys
in the other, I thought not this
time, as I held the buck's visage,
our eyes steadily trained on each
other, not even a single muscle
flinching in either one of us —
and my fully entering that zone
of timelessness in experiencing
being with an animal in the *wild*.
Except, finally, I was shocked
that it wasn't me, the human,
who moved first, and that,
actually, not only moved, but
regally strolled away with
a distinct toss of its head, as if
to indicate it had not the time
for these humans who stand
around, doing their own best
imitation of a placard, even
having the hubris to think they
know anything about deer,
since, let's get this straight
right now, it is deer that know
something about them, and
not the other way around.

The Mice of Fort Juniper

My favorite place to sit
    was at Robert Francis's round
        oak table, placed before the two front

windows, where I could look through
    tree branches to Market Hill Road,
        watch the first drops of that day's

summer rain begin to fall and bead
    on the windy parquet of green leaves.
        First the small piping noise seemed

to come out of the very air,
    an indecipherable Morse Code, which
        was not anything I could comprehend,

and even may have forgotten about,
    as its transmission resembled that
        of a satellite broadcasting its location

through incomprehensible space.
    Although the piping became more
        alarmed, not so much at a higher pitch,

but louder, increasing to what
    was a full squeak, more frequent,
        but also more of a cry for help than one

of possible aggression. So, when
    I stood up from the chair, my eyes roved
        the entire room, until at last they came

upon the pile of recycled newspapers
    stacked on a chair, and there on top
        of the pile of *Daily Hampshire Gazettes*

was the smallest of mice, looking up
    at me in its pleading voice, its thumb-
        sized body followed by the curl of its

long tail, resembling the distinct shape
    of a comma, giving you, the reader,
        and me, the writer, reason to pause.

Bending down to view it more closely,
    it raised its head even higher, the pitch
        of its squeaks acknowledging some

higher order; and I picked up the top
    newspaper by its corners with both
        hands, after opening the front door,

stepping ever so lightly, careful not to
    dislodge the mouse, which placed
        its trust in me, then tilted the paper

among the iris growing to the side
    of the stone stoop, and the mouse slid
        into blades of grass bent by the rain,

where it began to drink the drops that
    formed and fell, the mouse quenching
        its thirst, appreciative of the uncanny

freedom that living at Fort Juniper
    affords, knowing it as I do, since
        it is there where I had gained mine.

The Chakras, as Flower Essences

Indian Paintbrush

This is where the siddha and initiate rest.
It may be represented as alimentation,
but it is also where we make use of
what we have at hand. Viewed through
the lens of aesthetics, this is the place
of creative expression, of how you
relate to me and how I respond to you.

Pomegranate

When this red fruit is broken open, we see
that its chambers resemble the heart with
its ventricles, holding clusters of seeds.
Here we can be in sensual touch with each
other, as well as intuitively. It is where we
turn up the sexual heat, nourish and thrive in
the arms of another; with urgency, procreate.

Sunflower

As much as we desire power over each other,
horizontally, inflected vertically, we mine
our depths, tapping the inner ore; power up
the glimmering psychic metals that enable
us to cogitate clearly; joyfully engender
reason, purposefully gather strength; allow
the child within us, *Puer*, to dance.

Wild Rose

Jung thought he had climbed the trellis this
far, which is another way of saying this is
where the emanation of the Sacred Heart
of Jesus pulses with compassion, of love.

So, if you are feeling listless, find heirloom
roses within your own garden; enliven
yourself; inhale their being to start living.

Desert Larkspur

If you want to touch this spot, put your fingers
upon your throat, speak a word; you will come
to know how important it is to enunciate well,
to speak mindfully. In transition, as we all are,
it is here we find how to live. Here we divine
spiritual direction; we recalibrate our compass;
the lodestone of guidance points a new way.

Flower Aster

The delightful surprise is that this center is
between your eyes. This is where we develop
vision of another kind: not just what we can
normally see, but where we hone the planes
of illumination, forge insight's bright star.
Aligning our evolutionary paths, the lens of
wisdom, in its magnificence, is polished here.

Saguaro

Sarhasrara, purple crown, blossoms beyond
blossoms, where the myriad is One. Here we
see only footprints in the sand. We cleanse
in space that is galactic. The body's tension
relaxes; Kundalini rises up the spine, continues,
expands as a tuning fork's struck tone. We are
aware of the ringing of so many clear glass bells.

Trump

How can we not rail against the political
malfeasance of Donald Trump, which reveals

the dark underbelly of bigotry inherent
in America? His stance on immigration and

his condescending attitude towards Hispanics
bring the book *The Ugly American* to mind,

that quasi-*roman a clef*, regarding a particular
American insensitivity to another nation's

culture, which became such an influential
novel, that in 1958, Senator Kennedy

from Massachusetts gave a copy to every
colleague of his in the Senate. Who can

exhibit as much greed and be as loathsome
as Trump; who represents the conservative

malaise; whose claim that President Obama's
birth certificate is illegitimate illustrates

his own brand of racism; whose trademark
You're fired, portrays an oligarch's ostentation

and lack of humanity. If Trump invested
his millions in jobs for the homeless instead

of an inordinately expensive Grecian Formula
for his own ego, he might have diverted

his own disgrace and misplaced animosity.
With the rise of Donald Trump, we have

openly become laughable in the eyes
of the world. Trump's impertinent rhetoric

reflects only what some Americans think,
and it is just one reason why Muslim

women write *I hate America* in Arabic
on the fingers of their hands.

What a dreadful prospect it is to imagine
God Bless, America being sung

in conjunction with the American flag
flying behind an image of that financial

glutton and corporate monster, the reality
TV impresario, the politician as intolerant

bigot, the entrepreneurial predator with
the blowsy hairdo, who is Donald Trump.

— July 2015

Ode to My New Shoes

I first saw them on a rack
at Paul's Shoe Repair.
They called to me silently
the way someone who is
lonely does from the corner
of a room, but also like
someone who has much to say
of substance the cordovan
shoes offered me their glisten
and polish, their redness
emanating through the tone
of their brown gleam.
To understand their loneliness
further, Paul informed me
that someone had left them
behind after he made a repair
to them, and that is why
he was willing to let them go
at only $20. When I put them
on I felt elated by the quality
of their Florsheim Oxford
appeal. They made me feel
more than an inch taller
walking on their black soles
and stacked heels. Although
I needed to bring them back
to Paul so they could be
stretched and lifts cemented
inside both back quarters,
these cordovans accommodate
the bunion on my right foot
and the sensitive big toe
of my left, where I lost a nail

hiking in a boot that didn't
quite fit. I trust them
to carry me across any gallery
parquet, and hear them
speak their happy chatter
by their clicking echoing
never beneath me but
to each side, all around me,
in harmony with my gait,
making sure they alert me to
their unreserved joy that
their use is being implemented,
that I can depend on them
in all weather to carry me
over shiny flat surfaces and
the crunch of cinders when
crossing parking lots of uneven
ground, and that they will not
only be two of my daily
companions but will support
me in all that I do, cushion
my arches, protect all ten toes,
and offer me overall comfort
for my two feet, walking
with me stride for stride,
wherever it is I need to go.

An Act of Love

for Lisa Rappoport

The broadsides arrived today,
just moments ago. They look

delightful. Simple but elegant.
That blood red on that rich light

tan of the Fabriano Tiziano.
The lovely embellished ribbon

resplendent beneath the poem's
title. Your clear-eyed vision

engendering the precision of
the images in the poem just by

the sensual physicality of each
word handset along the length

and the width of the page.
What lusciousness for the eye.

As a master chef plates Haute
cuisine, you forever stylize

the depth of the printed word,
pressed firmly on the surface

of each leaf of paper, not so
removed from an act of love,

or that of forging the truth, as
in the intaglio of that blind-

stamped rose, which is etched
without ink, but that, as if

by the magic of your hand,
intimates such a deep rich color.

Suicide Vest

You will begin to see what you enter
is neither heaven nor is it certainly

paradise, and you will need to return
in order to make amends again;

and it will be necessary to see
and witness all of the pain you have

caused, the limbs you have severed,
the lives you could have loved

but instead just lost, the bodies burst
apart, which are now spatters on a wall.

How can we make it plain that
this is not the way to praise ourselves

or divinity, nor is it proper
to read a sacred text literally, since

jihad is just a metaphor and wasn't
meant to be taken as fact. The war

that was to be waged is to take place
within, so the heart can be cleansed

and made appropriate for the spirit
to move in and to flourish in a state

of peace where all is quiet and still
and not in terror or a palace of unease.

Make no mistake, for those who
decide to wear such a vile invention

and to pull the cord is anything but
glamorous or valiant, the act itself

of detonating such a device and
perpetrating such horror is inhumane,

and of such evil, and so much a crime,
that to take one's own life as an empty

sacrifice in such misplaced glory is in
direct opposition to what our legacy of

consciousness auspiciously portends,
but leaves a crater in the ground,

fatally taking those who are innocent,
with the perpetrator vanishing in such

heinous ignominy what remains is only
the darkness where hatred emanates.

Presence on the Mountain

At the fork,
    two miles up from the trailhead
      where you can continue to

circumnavigate the mountain
    or take the path to the summit,
      I saw them and they made me

pause, as the antlered buck
    crashed through the deadfall
      caught in the lower story

saplings, front legs tucked,
    keeping his head horizontal to
      the ground, back legs thrusting

in order to clear the way
    for the pregnant doe behind him,
      who also displayed her own

strength just by keeping up
    with the buck, the two of them
      at one with each other and in

their beauty by being just who
    they were, and they're not even
      noticing me standing to the side

of the screed washout dug deep
    after the heavy autumn rains, but
      they kept at it, crossing the low

ridge, until they were out
    of sight, allowing me to witness
      the revelation of their mystery.

To Where I Live

It has been my room of my own, my safe
house, my writer's studio, my atelier, my

gourmand's kitchen, rolled into one.
Many people actually react physically to

its size, and I observe their body language,
when they see where I live. My studio

is small but I have not only flourished
and prospered here but I have also experienced

the best days of my life during times
of just enough and even plenty,

the sunlight flooding through these seven
windows, not counting the glass door.

After reading Virginia Woolf's book
about her room of her own, I often

dreamed as a young man of having a place
in the country just like this, and even

imagined someone named *Jimmy* would
live above me, as there is living above me

now, which the synchronicity of electrifies
me every time I think about it. What this

studio has afforded me for over a decade
is that it has enabled me to live within

the landscape, in harmony with the land,
through its views of the world around me.

This has evidenced my needing to lead
an entirely new inspired life, and perhaps that

is best found and lived with humility in
a smaller space than a larger space. So, yes,

my studio is small, but most people don't
see it for what it is and for what it is worth.

It has been a priceless experience for me
to live where I am, among the meadows

and the tree break, amid the flyway
and foxes in the meadows, among what has

found its way into my heart and what has
streamed forth from within me.

Tzu-jan

Literally meaning
self-ablaze, it is what I experienced

standing in the riverbed of Cushman
Brook that summer of drought those

twenty-five years ago, my Labrador
standing on the banks, curiously

watching me, tilting her head side-
ways, my feet astride the dry rocky

streambed. *Tzu-jan*, a higher cosmic
order, wilderness ecology at its best,

burning through the true center
of being, in you, in me, in the dust,

now windblown, out across browned
meadow grasses that day I looked up,

stunned at my realization everything
perpetuated, all of it being nascent,

occurring in the moment of the ever
present now, each now anew,

refoliating as the massive winter
sycamores do each spring, branches

high above their camouflaged
bark, sprouting verdant green again,

its *self ablaze* throughout its height
and girth, having been replenished

by the sunlight, as the brook would be
with the hard rains later that August,

long after I would ascend its steep
slope up to where my Labrador

waited, tail wagging, our hearts set
afire with the utter rhapsody of

the single moment hovering before
us, magnificent in its splendor

within us, radiant heat emanating
from the dusty rocks and dry stones.

Grand Wizard

People lined the curb
along the length of Flagler Street —

Memorial Day, Miami, 1958,
I recall my mother holding my hand,

when I was five. The white summer
dress she sewed from a pattern made

only more fashionable with the blue silk
sash around her waist, and me dressed

in beige shorts, a green polo, sandals —
both of us delighting in the parade,

the colorful display of the marchers,
the onlookers. Until the wedge

of the white cloaked riders, with
veils and pointed hats, on horseback,

approached where we stood
on the side of the road; their energy

that of an imminent impenetrable
darkness drawing you into its center,

magnetically; and for everyone
to see, its Grand Wizard, his veil

lifted, hard obdurate eyes gazing
into the crowd along the street named

after the Standard Oil magnate and
railroad tycoon who died accidentally

in a fall down the marbled stairs of his
home at Whitehall. My boy's soul

intuited evil incarnate and rebelled
against it instantly, the sheer malice

and foul malevolence in the man's
visage, smoldering beneath the zany

hoodlum costume, precipitating
my protest beside my mother, openly

crying out that I didn't like that man,
the one on horseback riding past us,

the man meeting my face with his cold
eyes, the one my mother began pulling

me away from and covering my mouth,
beginning to make her way through

the crowd by the curb with me
in tow, her stopping eventually to

whisper loudly to me that I couldn't
say such things out loud to the man

on the horse, that he could do
things to us that we would not want

done, that he and his men were
the ones who burned crosses on front

lawns, that these horseback riders
were known as the Ku Klux Klan.

Distance

What I remember most
about the drive north to Connecticut from Miami

is the blueness of the rainy evenings;
the stopping at diners for our meals, fragrant

with coffee, burgers, and fries; flipping through
the selections on the jukebox, the rhythms

of the Doo-wop beating in time with the raindrops
striking the windows of our booth, Sinatra's voice

soothing the poignance of the storm;
then there was the smell of mothballs and bibles

filling the emptiness of motel room drawers;
my father visibly aching from the long drive,

my mother's interminable patience that everything
would all work out when we arrived in Milford

to reconnect with friends, to visit with her cousins
in Ansonia, worrying that she needed to enroll me

in parochial school before the school year began;
intuiting the need to finish things before her

unexpected collapse from the cerebral hemorrhage,
to die six days later on the operating table;

leaving behind a son immersed in the amber
of catatonia, a husband who would wear his

bereavement as he would bear a wound; however
it was in our driving beneath the hanging Spanish

moss in Georgia when we passed a chain gang
in their red and white stripes that I met the gaze

of an African-American man with an animated
face, quizzically meeting my eyes, looking out

the backseat window; his expression intimating
to me how much he wanted to be unchained again,

to be able to put down his pickaxe and to get out
of the heat, to quit the punishing road work

of breaking stones, to throw off the gravity
of the iron weighing down his limbs, and as our

car continued up the road, to climb in with us,
to release himself from his captivity, to revel

in seeing the distance accrue into the magnitude
of the passing landscape, the stark glassiness

of his eyes staying with me all of these years,
the pleading in them, his dire face expressing

the dread I would come so well to know myself
that openly relayed please don't leave me behind.

Wandering, Mazily

Neruda writes
that he will *wander mazily over all the earth*
if his lover leaves him.

He importunes her that
her shadow never disappears into distance on
the beach; and his joy

in love, even in the sorrow
that such connection with another portends,
is not anything that exists

in my life at this time; but
I am filled with Neruda's mazily wandering
across the momentous sands

of time, as I trod over
the black and gray stones of the driveway in
mud season, soldiering

on in my solitary life,
in my often obscure or sometimes confused
fashion, unaware of

how blue the cloudless
sky is, its reflection replicated in the luminous
puddles of mud, set

with the glitter of wet
stones; knowing as I do that neither I, nor you,
is obscure, as confused

as we might be, occasionally
made all that much larger by our wayward
diversions in following our

soul's journey, under whose
blue sky we might finally realize is filled
by a night that is lit by

an infinite number of stars,
whose light shines long after their deaths,
whose departures are as

perpetual as their eternal
essence, since what has never been born
never truly dies, since it is as

inviolate as what streams forth
from what may even be oblique, which
sparkles as mazily as any star.

Angels of the Night

I found two giant leopard moths, who were, apparently,
joined in mating, on the porch this morning, after

the violent wind and rain of last night's thunderstorm.
White teardrop wings, each about two inches long;

although one was larger than the other,
and it may have been the male; grub-like underneath,

with the wings speckled with dark splotches.
They were linked in their being absolute: beautiful

and monstrous at the same time — their death, sublime,
the two of them connected like that. Initially, I thought

it was just one massive four or five inch long insect,
until I turned them over and they fell apart in my hands.

They were remarkable, sad, momentous angels
of the night,as in D. H. Lawrence's *Women in Love*,

when Doctor Brindell is found with Diana Crich,
both drowned, and the woman's hands wrapped around

the man's neck. Although it is not the same:
to find Shelley on that beach near Viareggio, his body

wound in strands of seaweed, also possessed
that otherwordly and ghoulish sense of awe and dread.

from

The View of the River

(2017)

Deer Park

after Wang Wei

Solitary, on the mountain;
deep in the forest, no one for miles —

although, the voices from the valley
rise up in the distance.

Returning, to cast shadows, late sun
breaks through the pine branches.

Reappearing again, the light illumines
the moss, as green as jade reflections.

Long Mountain

When I look up at Long Mountain,
easternmost promontory of the Holyoke Range,

it is merely a ridge to what it must have been
when prehistoric Lake Hitchcock

pooled upon its shores when the flood plain
was immersed in the waters of a glacier

millennia ago. *Worn down by the wind and the rain,*
I think, and look back up,

never-ending to be mesmerized
by the mystery that its slopes hold through each

season and during any
weather — just as is sorrow diminished by time.

Skiers

after Robert Francis

They unroll strokes in a scroll of incandescent
calligraphy down the slope,

flaring white powder behind them across the blue
snow shadow of the mountain.

The sibilance of their skis only increases the quiet
within them as they write their signatures

in the weave of the slalom
in their descent, leaving behind them the sound of

the wind in the pines.
They finish in a flourish, the blades of their skis

cutting grooves into
the snow crust as they brake their motion in wide

arcs at the bottom,
taking their entire run down with them as they might

spangle a ribbon in
its many arcs, in not only an act of strength but also

to exhibit what is essential —
a resplendent aesthetic; pure form in a cold world

of white on white; agility then speed in a display
of inner fire, sheer release.

Snowy Owl

When one winter dusk I saw you land
on the peak of the cinderblock garage,

as I glanced out the front door,
almost perfect, perched on the brim

of the shingled roof, you tantalized me
by your otherworldly ghost

manifestation, haunting hunter,
phantom apparition, feathers fluttering

in the fading light.
When on sub-zero nights you return

to call from the row of windbreak pines,
your call pervading me,

setting me free to fly with you,
who swoops and rises again in the icy wind,

who practices the precision of fight, whose
golden corneas, menacing angel, illumine the dark.

Fox

She travels the border on this side
of the windbreak of farm and open meadow and,

between the time I look out the front window,
place my bowl of soup on the table, lift my head again,

moves, releases herself to the wind, springs on
black-furred feet so quick, so deliberate

in the rhythm of graceful bounds, her light red coat,
stretched full length, the white bib of her chest barely

visible in its invisibility. I am left breathless by
the four leaps that take her to an opening among

clumps of leafless honeysuckle where she slips
into dusk, turning silver as she springs, rapturous,

into mind, into body, this everlasting
moment passing as it passes into the miraculous.

Heart's Essence

*The heart is not human that does not love. There is no use
in denying the fact that happiness or misery is, somehow,
strangely connected with the connections of the heart.*

> an underlined passage in *The Romance of Abelard and
> Heloise*, by O. W. Wight, page 13 (New York: Appleton,
> 1853), a book found in Emily Dickinson's bedroom

What connections of the heart draw us together, Emily,
on this day that will too soon be forgotten,
the rhododendron hedge flowering pink between your
lawn and your brother, Austin's; a festival of buttercups
beneath oak and shagbark hickory.

What a buzz of silence there is behind
these ivory-colored lace curtains; your white linen dress
on display next to your chair and writing table;
a lamp you might have used on the second floor looking
west on Main Street in Amherst.

What hope this fresh wallpaper offers
with green stems and leaves, whose arbors support such
a rich color of the rose, alembic of the heart's essence,
that it pacifies the mind and invites repose —
constancy being no simple thing,

as your devotion to poetry exemplifies.
However, is this not how we are connected through such
diligent practice that both flower and fruit
are indicative of the harvest of our own expansiveness
and transcendence; our own poetic alchemy converting

boons from loss, grace from discontent;
whetted by the intoxicating elixir
of the lubricant of the auspiciously written word,
the ones that defy gravity and lift
off the page in their own light; and hover there.

Ode to Presence

I made a healing soup today:
crushing cloves of garlic, carving up

onions, chopping the resilient stalks
of scallions, julienning the bells

of Holland peppers, cutting rounds
of carrots, and briskly slicing celery,

which I sauté in olive oil in the thick-
bottomed pot, accompanied with

cumin, thyme, and turmeric, also
known as the princess of the kitchen,

and a pinch of red pepper flakes.
I add the basmati rice, minced

parsley, morsels of leftover chicken
trimmed and scraped from the bones

of the carcass before I used it to
make stock. After each step,

I smiled, and didn't need to ask
myself if I was happy, finding

a rhythm in each small task, every
step in preparing this chicken

and rice soup, made with delight,
not concerned with the aches in

my aging body, the burn of my
bunions, the stiffness in the lower

back, the ever constant tiredness
which attends to my best efforts

at presence. That was all mitigated
by my making the soup with care,

a buoyant joy, with no thought
of yesterday, nor of tomorrow, just

the fullness of the moment, which
always expands with the attention

you bring to it; and when I take
the vat of soup off the burner

of the stove to cool, and then to
refrigerate it so that its flavors will

meld overnight, I am pleased
by the fragrance of the medley

of vegetables, the blend of chicken
and rice, which will sustain me

for days and nights to come, that
will remind me of the satisfaction

of having spent an afternoon
making soup, which will continue

to offer me fulfillment of purpose,
and to heal me with its nourishment.

Porcupine

My Labrador loved Saturday mornings,
knowing that day of the week was the one

I would spend more time with her than
any other, the sliding glass door open

on a mild day in May, that sweet transom
between spring and summer, when

her *woof* led me out of the kitchen to see
what held her attention, nose pressed into

the screen, and there the bristled porcupine
quivered in its intensity, quills

flaring from its coat like an arsenal of spines,
body the size of a piglet

or a small dog. I quickly took hold
of my Labrador's collar, so she wouldn't go

right through the bulge she had made in
the mesh, and slid the glassed door closed,

since just beyond the other side of the porch
the rotund animal's waddle had come

to a halt, and it glared
at us from its pinioned shawl, its flat porcine

nose working to
pick up our smell, black eyes glinting with

annoyance and dread,
as if we intruded on its own existence —

it barked once, trundling past the window
to the barn, and into open meadow,

to the reach of the bracken, the lance
of its impression caught

in our collective memories, the tether hooks
of their shafts never quite pried loose.

Finding My Grandfather

There is the photograph
of my father's father in military uniform,
an Austrian, serving in the Polish cavalry
in World War I, standing ramrod straight.

It is he whom I think of when
I find myself dowsing my genome for
answers regarding my origin, the deep
pull that draws me to the late symphonies

of Mozart, Rilke's angelic mysticism, and,
as a child, to *Krapfen* and *Apfelstrudel*.
However, how could I ever discount
the perpetual awe I find in Chopin's *Etudes*

and the wonder of the first and second
piano symphonies, the lyrical madness
in the short stories of Bruno Schulz.
That grandfather died shortly after returning

to his farm from the results of having been
a victim of a mustard gas attack in the war.
There are no photographs
of my mother's father, who it is said I am

a namesake, since she never fully recovered
from his premature death in an automobile
accident in New Jersey while driving home
in his Model-T Ford one stormy evening,

the spokes of two of the spinning wheels
splashing with falling rain as the car lay
on its side, overturned in a roadside ditch.
This was the grandfather who I heard

was beloved, and was referred to as being
reciprocal of such love in return. This
grandfather leaves no image from which I can
gaze, only the darkness from which he drank.

There needs not to be a photograph for
the grandfather I did have, known as Grandpa
Gorski, whom my mother's mother married
after the death of her *Waju*. This man I would

come to know as a boy of three, until he died,
three years later, when I had arrived at my full
precocity at the age of six. This grandfather
was not a true grandfather but more of one than

any of the others, the one who was the reconciler,
the steady one who intervened with wisdom,
who provided calm to the warring factions of my
father and grandmother, who resided in a house

of hysterics. I remember finding resolute trust
in this man in whom I recognized equanimity.
Moments before his death, he called for me,
and my grandmother took me to see him in their

room, so he could hear my playing ukulele for
him, a smile spread on his face beneath
the darkened circles around his eyes. How I can
still feel the hand he placed on my head, briefly,

before removing it, whereupon, he vacated
the body he had in that life, and, at least in my
imagination, arose into the storm winds that filled
the hurricane that ravaged the Floridian sky.

The Streaming

Rain light, late November —
the pippins remaining on branches

in the orchard
in the shadow of the mountain,

glowing, nearly translucent;
each lozenge a struck tone

when the long beams
of early morning emerge above

the slopes of the treeline of conifer
that then distinguishes

such evanescence, another becoming,
the melting frost, every droplet

of dew; always this
gift of the lucid memory

of someone's hand,
dear to you, once touching yours.

After Long Drought

The sky rips open
after days of grinding heat,
waves of meadow grass

shift in the blowing rain,
and floating on the breadth
of its extended wings,

as bright as a vision,
the great blue heron
strokes through the storm.

Lloyd

The angry voices from the gray ranch
were loud enough to echo throughout

the neighborhood, and I had managed
to extricate myself from the confines

of the house, choosing to sit with
my head in my hands on the curb.

They were at it again —
my stepmother Marcella, who doesn't

deserve to be immortalized in a poem,
and Fred, my father, whom I would

find out was suffering from Alzheimer's
on my twenty-first birthday. You could

hear dishes and glasses breaking against
a wall from the street. They had

a special spot in the dining room that
they would choose to throw China

and crystal, where there was a palate
of color from all of the food that

splattered against their target in
the Dada of their rage. Whatever they

accused me of doing, and for what
incremental offense, they threatened

the honor student who wanted to go to
Choate with sending him to Cheshire

Reformatory. What surprised me was
how the sound of them in there traveled

and how clearly you could hear their
every word, the vitriol of their contempt

for each other and life itself seeping into
the balm of an otherwise delightful

early spring evening. This is when
Lloyd came over to me beside the curb,

our neighbor next door, whose garage
was always filled with a collection of

adding machines from his job as a
salesman with National Cash Register,

on which he supported his wife and
four children. Rumor had it that Lloyd

had lost his job and he was suffering
from a breakdown, but he sat down

next to me on the curb and placed one
of his large arms around my shoulders

to console me. He quietly told me he
understood, and that things wouldn't

always be this way for me, that they
would change for the better, and that

I would be able to leave one day.
His presence filled me as if God, or

one of the angels, had come to buoy
me up from drowning in my own

sorrow; and he sat there with me until
night fell, not saying much, but

making certain to make me feel better,
having offered me from his very

depths the salve of assuagement and
the ointment of consolation,

the fragrance of the lawns blending
with that of the cooling dark macadam.

The View of the River

It was the view of the river
   that intrigued me, that lured me
      toward its banks, the sheer

vastness of its panorama, as I
   looked north, the sheen on its
      surface, which broke then

broke again in the choppiness
   of its waves that September
      morning my mother was

interred into the earth forever,
   as I lost myself among
      headstones in the graveyard,

presupposed to be standing
   along with my father, aunt,
      uncle, and grandmother beside

the open grave, but instead
   chose to wander, intuiting
      both my new freedom, which

reflected itself in the water
   of the flowing river, river
      that empowered the factory

towns of the impoverished
   Connecticut Valley, known
      as the Housatonic, its brown-

silver muddiness carrying
    itself to the sea, and what was
        my incomprehensible loss

due to my mother's death,
    which seared itself into
        my psyche with an intaglio

that would perennially ink
    itself with her memory.
        There I stood, and heard

my name being called as I
    teetered high on a ledge
        above the Housatonic,

gazing upriver, magnetized
    by a destiny I could not
        either interpret or imagine,

the coolness of the river's
    rush emanating up the bank,
        its turbulence caught on its

own swirling eddies, the gritty
    odor of it as it propelled
        forward out of the Valley,

away from the tedium of
    the hiss and bang of machines
        in the manufacturing plants

and their medieval domination
of the workers enslaved within
the brick walls, resembling

fortresses or prisons,
the river calling me as my life
summoned me, while needing

to listen to the voices which
urged me toward them, among
the tombstones, which I began

to run towards, all the while
carrying the vision of the river
within me, which still courses

and churns in its archetypal
flow, surging onward, that
always reminds me, and never

lets me forget, what heartache
is, as I listen to it pound
within upon its bed of stones.

Cinema

The first film I remember seeing was
The Rat Race, with Tony Curtis and Debbie Reynolds, a blur
of a memory, sitting next to my mother, who I believe was
her way of preparing me, at the age of eight, for the society

I would eventually enter, and honoring the intuition of her
death. I recall how she grasped me close next to her in
the seat beside her, only days later would she vacate her body
and leave this world, with grave inimitable solemnity.

When I saw *Doctor Zhivago*, I knew I had something;
the mother's death at the beginning of the film, and the scene
with Zhivago passing Lara in the trolley, before they had
ever met, and the sparks that ignited above the carriage, over

their heads, will be with me forever, never mind the mysterious
afterglow about their faces, when they are shown in bed
together, baffling my twelve-year old nature; but it was when
Zhivago was writing the Lara poems by candlelight in

the snow mansion, balling up early drafts and tossing them
on the floor, now that sung to me as what I could do with my life.
Although it wasn't until the summer after high school,
when I would begin to see films twice, once for enjoyment, and

the second time for critical effect, that I stayed several times for
The Sting, with Paul Newman and Robert Redford; or when
I was reading Hermann Hesse, and saw *Steppenwolf*, with
Max von Sydow, that film began to become art, upon

which I referred to such productions as cinema, and my joining
four film societies at Yale, my favorite being the one at
the Law School, where on Saturday nights there were always big
films being shown, such as Fellini's *Casanova*, with Donald

Sutherland, looming large on the screen, black cape dragging
the ground behind him, or Lina Wertmuller's *Seven Beauties*,
and Giancarlo Giannini who expanded the definition of tragic-
comic hero of the silver screen, as irritating and sometimes

cowardly as he was often handsome and endearing.
Not until Wim Wenders' masterpiece *Wings of Desire*, or
Der Himmel Uber Berlin, shot by Henri Alekan, who also was
the cinematographer for Jean Cocteau, and who provided

the grain of the black and white scenes by using a remnant
of his grandmother's silk stockings from the 1930s. This film
being the definition of what cinema can be, reflecting upon
my own life and its myth and fairy tale *assemblage*, written

by Peter Handke, often giving the actors lines sounding as if
they might have been written by Rilke; with Bruno Ganz, who
abdicated his immortal angelhood by throwing down his angelic
breastplate for the nubile trapeze artist, Marion, played by

Solveig Dommartin, true and perennial *erdengel*; how you must
look down on us now from your heavenly nimbus, having died
too young. If we are so very lucky, in our hours of alarm, should
we awaken to find around our mortal shoulders your dear arms.

Eulogy

for Jerry Gafio Watts

My first memory of you has to be
that of your hands combing through
the sale books on the cart in front
of the store one autumn afternoon

in 1975, your brown leather brief-
case, with a gold metal latch, your
Ce que vous êtes connu par. That
was your first year in New Haven,

having just graduated from Harvard,
and you wearing the poor Ph.D.
student persona as well as you did
that Walt Frazier mustache; although

you never grew an Afro, your hair
was always well groomed, like that
of Malcolm or Stokley Carmichael.
Too poor to buy books, you read

standing up, and if you didn't finish
you would come back the next day
and pick up where you had left off.
However outspoken you might have

been, you deflected praise for
the street people you would put up
in your small apartment on sub-
zero nights. Your heart always

matching the largesse of your good
Samaritan acts, including the time
I was broken into when I was living
over on the Hill, and you insisted on

accompanying me when I returned
to gather my things. When we
managed the bookstore on Saturday
nights, your students would sit on

the floor below the raised counter,
where you would hold court, lecture
them about American studies and
W.E.B. DuBois. Two decades later,

when we found ourselves both on
another college campus in Hartford,
you included me in the dedication
to your magnum opus, *Amiri Baraka:*

The Politics of the Black Intellectual,
where you honored our collegiality.
When I found out about your death
last November, on your birthday this

May, I comprehended the synchronicity
to be all about your thinking it was
about time that I should finally know.
How could we realize there might be

forty years ahead of us when we first
met, as you were perusing the titles on
that cart of books I had wheeled out
on the street, knowing as I do now that

I'll never not stop perceiving your sharp
inflection when I recall hearing
you say, *Brothah, how are you doin',*
Brothah, while being aware that we

actually were kinsman of the heart,
and how if we were informed that we
might have had four decades to read
and write we would have smiled and

thought ourselves fortunate, but how
those years have elapsed so quickly
that I would have wanted to share with
you how I believe we just might have

discovered something valuable about
our experience in how the evanescent
is a necessary component in
the divine creation of what is *éternité*.

Cameo

It is not so much who she is,
as Poirot suggested about the unidentified
dead body in *The Clocks*, but
who she is, which can confuse almost any-

one, if we aren't paying attention.
As your cameo role in my life did when we
met, you as my third grade teacher, and I
as your student, who had just

lost his mother. Was it the opportunity to
clean erasers and blackboards
after school that I had volunteered for so
I wouldn't need to arrive home

to the flat devoid of a mother's love? Or
did I really feel your reaching out
to me and that opening led me to unfurl
my child's soul to you, so much

so that you invited me to your room in
the convent next door to
Saint Michael's, where, as you informed
me after our discussion of

death, you kept a human skull atop your
dresser, which you said
became your focus of meditation so that
you could have a greater

understanding of death, and in so doing
you might live life more fully.
Your suggestion piqued my curious boy's
mind, and we arranged our

after school appointment the way some
lovers arrange their tryst —
covertly from public view, although openly
between themselves. As you

led me down the long hallway, hand in hand
to your room, I didn't
expect you to invite me to sit on your bed,
upon which the corners

of the covers were tucked in with military
precision. As I rested myself down,
I remember the tautness of the blankets,
as if I were sitting on a cloud, and

as your sister nuns walked passed, some of
whom looked in briefly, soft smiles
playing across their faces, as if they may have
intuited that there was as much

sensuality about this event as there was any
amount of metaphysical investigation
regarding the subject of death and dying as
evidenced in the skull on the bureau

opposite me, which held my rapt attention
more than the epiphanal experience of
being in Sister's room and my anxiousness
in my hoping she would return so

I could ask her questions about the skull, so
I wouldn't have to divert any more
of her colleagues' glances as more of them
seemed to find reason to pass by

than before, and what if Mother Superior had
found out about this foray into
the house of the divine feminine by her young
nun and a student? However, you

did return, as lovers do, who eventually leave
again, but who are remembered
more for the intensity of their relationship than
for its brevity; and I recall you

saying we couldn't stay long since you might
be bending the house rules, but
I will never forget that you, indeed, did and
that whatever infatuation danced

between us is still choreographed in my heart,
so many decades later, that I thank
you for showing me the way toward what I
recall as a sweetness in realizing

a reason for being, feeling an unexpected wind
rippling the silkiness of our life, the way
the early morning coolness has
in whetting the beginning of a summer's day.

Green Herons

for Bob Abel

1   We meet at the trailhead of the Conte Reserve,
    the weather this August morning not cool

    but overcast and clement, with the humidity
    only becoming noticeable when we near

    the Fort River, its muddy shoals prominent and
    green with blades of grass in a drought summer.

2   We talk only about things that matter:
    you mention how you recently spotted a blue-

    winged warbler and comment how these thick
    alder woods are favorable for sighting one.

    I point out jimsonweed growing in a bower
    and mullein lavishing on the sandy flats,

    with its basil leaves and those creamy-yellow
    blossoms starring its tall stems.

3   Joe-pye weed rises above of a tangle of brush
    beyond the wooden pavilion on the path;

    along the cinder trail a baby rabbit appears,
    undisturbed by two humans whose strides

    crunch with each step of their boots. When
    we come to the outlook of open meadow,

    which stretches to a tree break before bordering
    the ridges of the Holyoke Range, we can see

the mist rising through the rain on the slopes of
the Seven Sisters, just like in a Chinese scroll.

4   You become quiet and I cease talking,
as we near the detritus of deadfall on the banks

of the deadwood bog. You raise your
binoculars, and say in a whisper, *Green heron*,

as the bird majestically skitters the length of
a fallen trunk of white pine. Shyly, it appraises

us, but is still comfortable with the distance
between us, shifting from one leg to another,

bolting quickly, again, from bank to log, and
back again, then moving cautiously out of sight.

5   As we finish the walk, it has
stopped raining, and the meadows are alive with

Queen-Anne's lace highlighted with blue chicory.
Shifting from foot to foot, the green heron steps

lightly along flotsam of pine in the deadwood bog,
mingling with all of its brethren

whom we did not see but who were ardently
peering at us through their veil of viridescence.

from

The Map of Eternity

(2017)

Ode to the Holyoke Range

From the expanse
of farm meadows on Moodybridge Lane,

that still hasn't been ruined
by more thoughtless development,

a complete vista can be seen in its particular
splendor. This series of hills could be

an installation sculpture of a landlocked
school of cresting baby belugas

rising across the sky
from right to left, and west to east.

These 200 million year old basalt mountains
worn by weather and time,

snow and ice glazing their cliff faces well into
early spring, annually revivify themselves —

as the Japanese haiku poet Tadashi Kondo
once said to me, "They are most beautiful now,

with the lime green blossoms of budding trees,
infusing the contours of the ridges,

making them at least as beautiful
as the crimson and yellow colors of autumn."

The five distinct peaks: Mt. Holyoke,
Mt. Hitchcock, Bare Mt., Norwottuck, and

Long Mountain, whose views include
the diminutive Fort River Valley ecosystem,

and whose irregular plateau looks down on
its rocky upper slopes that blaze in the sun;

whose lower ravines remain cool
and moist, folded into the shade of its cliffs;

defines where I have lived for most of my life,
has me measuring the length of each day

by observing the seasonal changes
of weather that pass over its slopes,

impacting my very existence, inculcating
a humility and gratitude of living —

in cultivating an appreciation of what is
worn, what is known as *wabi*, in Japanese;

and what is both timeless and finite in its
distinct and boundless hardscrabble iterations.

Woodland Frogs

I will always remember the first time
I heard it —

that soft, wet rustling, which made me
think it was a large animal roving

through the bracken. However it was
of more enormous stature than

a single hulking creature, since
the mass exodus of the species made

their way through the already dewy
grass, traversing the meadow toward

the roadside pond, magnetized by
the hypnotic moon-reflected water.

From where I sat on the front
porch stoop of the apartment in

the barn, savoring the air of an April
evening, the mass evacuation

of them startled me into an astonish-
ment, as I quietly stared into

the darkness of the grass, shifting
with their springing through that

wetness, with their leaping over each
other, one after another, in such

an amphibian horde that it elicited
amazement at the veracity of their

mission. It precipitated awe in
the sheer dimension of the force

of their making the grassy darkness
shush in a slippery vernal migration.

Mesmerized with wonder, I watched
as the first ones leapt and dove into

the pond edge, splashing beyond
the reeds, breaking and re-breaking

that watery surface, as the throng
of them only made the moonlight

appear larger in its sheen, teeming
the surface with their prodigiousness,

as more and more of them flooded
in together to raise their voices

in a chorus, as if to match the watery
shine of lunar reflections, as they

sang for all their life, throbbing
with such aqueous rhythms, shrill

in their crying — this song of
the woodland frog, high-pitched

and quavering, often cresting, then
stopping and starting in waves —

nature's true falsetto, vocalizing
an impassioned celebratory trilling,

the piercing vibrancy of peepers
peeping in ponds in the spring.

Sun Worship

To speculate that there is no
sentience within the animal

kingdom is to cast oneself in
a net of sublime ignorance,

and if proof of a higher order
needs any substantiation then

the early autumn morning
I quietly stepped over the red

brick esplanade around which
surrounds half the farmhouse

to bring the recycling out to
the barn, I was stopped by

the spectral presence of
the milk snake that had lived

near the concrete porch steps
to the mud room. Elegantly

curled in several loops, half-
way down the cold parquet of

the walk, the snake faced east,
where the sun was already

rising over the ridges of
Mt. Orient, with its striated

red reflections glistening in
Lawrence Pond. There are

moments which open forever
and remain with us in their

quintessential nature, etched
as on a plate within our psyche,

as with this snake's head held
high, straight up from the draped

cursives of its body, statuesque,
steady in its gaze of the sunrise

over the eastern hills, that I felt
intrusive in its presence, not

wanting to interrupt such
magnificence, the rarity of

experience of viewing anything
so inviolate as another animal

in awe of the wonder of what is
sacrosanct in celebrating and

honoring the rising of the sun,
that how could I possibly

even bear to interrupt its sense
of worship, which could only,

with active humility,
increase an appreciation of mine.

Gothic

The last three weeks have knuckled my health
into a perversion. First there was the head cold;
then that moved to my chest; on the heels of that

was the left foot ankle sprain; after that gout
inflamed both feet. I ache for being well again
and I long for my walking every morning.

Living alone is one thing, but feeling like one
is an invalid is entirely another. That is not
necessarily self-pity. It is the truth. Women

normally have a safety network. Single old men
have none. Most people they have known, in
one way or another, have nearly forgotten them.

If you can't keep your health nothing remains.
I can walk, but, even after taking care of myself,
I am only the worse off for it. I can't remember

when I wanted winter to end as much as I do
this year. It has been a nasty season of shirtsleeve
weather one day and below zero wind chill the next.

I have never heard March gusts rage as much
as they have this year. They have been Trumpian
in their seething up and through the morass, then

across the sky. Forgive me for casting this
Poe-like mood of dusk settling over the darkest of
tarns. There is something Gothic about being ill.

Doors creak when they didn't creak before. Wind
blows brush over great swaths outside one's window.
The gnarly cold blows thinly through invisible

cracks in walls. One's bones ache and one's mind
is swathed in what appears to be eternal nightfall.

The Map of Eternity

I want to go back.
I want to go back to that one day in 1961,

just before my mother's death
when we walked to the luncheonette in

Ansonia on a hot day in early September.
The soda fountain sporting

three plastic dispensers whirling cold fruit
drink colors of orange, lemonade, and purple

grape. The mouthwatering fragrance of
beef burgers and hand-cut French fries.

The metallic gleam of the swivel stools
with their red plastic tops shining above

the black and white art deco design
of the patterned linoleum floor. Sunlight

filling the large plate glass windows,
their blinds raised to the view of the street.

My mother always seeming more tired
than ever these last days before the cerebral

hemorrhage, even achingly heavy-lidded,
so much so that I could feel her pain

of the constant headaches — not vicariously,
but palpably. However, this was a day

of grace, putting out a long thin tuber
of memory, whose off-white root can be

visible all these decades later. How it has
grown to connect that day to this one, this

day in which I rediscover that day,
ever so timelessly, in its own perpetuity:

cinematic and indelible in its reminiscence.
My recollection of telling my mother

in more of a question than a statement
what I thought I might be when I grew up,

and her dismissing my becoming a priest
just by her unusual silence; but as we

continued to walk back to the apartment
a day or two before her death, and my

starting parochial school, it was as if we
strode through the map of my life as it

would unfold for the next year without
her: Jack Kennedy's motorcade driving

through the center of town, the music
store where I would take guitar lessons

and make my first and only performance
of "Turkey in the Straw," the spires

of Saint Michael's and the red brick
school building in which I would labor

with grammar, maths, and my grief
in having lost a mother — such an open-

ended void and inexplicable morass —
how could I have had any idea, as I

do now that we were actually
also walking through an expanding

moment of the ineffable, one in which
I would come to be aware that

the map of eternity was only beginning
to spread out in all directions.

Hydrangea

These deciduous plants adorn
the lawns on which they lavish panicles,

large white flowerheads, growing
among spear-shaped evergreen leaves.

The bushes are as showy as their flowers
that are often thought

to resemble pom-poms.
Every spring and summer, I observe

their enormous blossoms bob among
their greenery as if noticing

someone one hasn't seen for however long
and whose name is momentarily gone,

as I forget their names every season.
The flowers bloom steadily through

midsummer into August lushness,
then begin their pink

blush in the late summer coolness
among the first harbingers

of the frosts of autumn.
Each year the flowers are dried and sold

on roadside stands to celebrate the turning
of the great wheel of summer.

And each year I finally remember, then forget
until next season, when the hydrangea

bloom so whitely, while my memory slips
away ever so much from year to year, until

it maybe lapses entirely:
Hydrangea, may I remember your name,

as I might inhale your spicy fragrance;
may I recall in winter

the murmur of your petals
whispering on the summer wind.

Rilke, at Chateau de Muzot

How you must have moved
with such abundant
grace between the two
writing desks Nanny
Wunderly sent to you

at the Chateau de Muzot,
in Veyras —
the one on which you finished
The Duino Elegies, the first
desk delivered;

and the second sent
by your patron because
she was unsure the first ever
arrived, upon which you wrote
the Orpheus sonnets.

How you must have moved
in that February light between
one desk and another, beneath
the postcard of Orpheus tacked up
by your current lover, Baladine

Klossowska, your inspiration —
leaving you alone to compose
in such enviable solitude.
As you wrote the mother
of the dead young dancer,

whom you dedicated
the sonnets to, Wera
Ouckama Knoop's ghost
was *commanding and
impelling you.*

How chilling, how vital
that must have been to hear Wera's
voice calling out to you, whispering,
as if she were Eurydice and you
were her Orpheus.

How you must have danced
from one desk to another as
a hurricane of the spirit blew
through your inner
thread and webbing.

How you must have held Eurydice
in your arms, then heard Wera calling
as you awakened each morning,
as an angel might, as we
now listen and are held by you.

Branta

October turns to November
and the golden light silvers.

They announce themselves as
they reappear

over the rim of the far meadow,
rearrange their wedge

in mid-flight. To hear
once more their voices,

the wild music of their cries,
their name, *Branta*,

a dialect native only to
their own. They fly

ragged in the wind, reform
across the sky —

then pause between
looking and listening, before they

disappear in air
I saw them stroking through

just now, a quietude settling,
until another flock

passes. Their lamentation
lingers

each day as they pass
and the season augurs toward winter.

Poem after James Wright's "In Fear of Harvests"

It still happens now, James.
As ever, somewhere, close by,
Nearly motionless, a solitary
Horse grazes, breath steaming
From its nostrils, as it snorts
Happiness.
And, yes, the bees, those
Ardent little sisters, work
The crops in the fields
And ply their small bodies
Into wreaths of blossoms,
Whose nectar thickens
Into wild honey
Beneath the buzz of silence,
As your words do,
In an apiary submerged
Beneath hives of snow.

The Veil

High blue September sky,
    the trail around
        the mountain, morning

leaf shadows
    on scree, remnants of
        an abandoned sugar shack,

burnt scent
    of autumn drifting,
        leaf-edges not quite

color-tinged.
    Shadow of the mountain's
        south face: a grove white

with boneset, more boneset
    than I have ever seen,
        flowerheads dense above

lance-shaped leaves,
    brightness fired by
        their own petals. Above

a red-tailed
    hawk on an oak
        branch, wary but content,

undaunted by
    my presence.
        He swivels his head

side to side,
      blinks his golden
            corneas, his piercing

black pupils.
      Breast feathers
            white like the boneset,

flecked with rust.
      I stand beneath,
            part of this wild veil,

drift away dazed,
      that sweet glimmering
            a memory to fill the years.

Augury

I found the corpse just above Salinas
on Route 101 in some tall scrub grass,

nearly intact, at the edge of the highway,
and stepped into a realm of the sublime,

even the *swoosh* of the trucks driving
past was muffled, as I saw the owl's

breast feathers blowing in the back draft.
I wanted to pick up its body and take it

with me, put it in my pack, but
that would have disturbed whatever pact

I might have made at the time with
what is sacred. Not even ants had made

their way into the relic of its body.
It must have been flying at night

and was blinded by headlights, struck
a windshield, and bounced off, just

beyond the breakdown lane. Looking
at its perfect body, as I leaned over it,

from where I was hitchhiking,
it appeared that I was able to see into

my own life, barely twenty, with its own
destiny of beauty and sorrow, the women

I would love and lose, the exigencies
that moved me toward the calling

of the spirit, the eventuality of my being
alone as an old man, all there

in the black and white speckled feathers
on its breast, bordered with russet ones;

the tufted ears, and the open eyes
that looked into the reliquaries of forever.

The Sunflowers

Their large heads loomed above me,
arrayed with their bright yellow petals.

Row after row of them arranged
in lines to the right side of the house

and adjacent to the garage in the back.
At nine, I looked up at their creaking

stalks on autumn days on my way to
and from school, and looked down

on their ranks from the glassed-in
porch of the second floor railroad flat

my father rented after my mother's
death. I was overcome by their yellow

brilliance and the size of their corollas,
which exceeded the diameter

of a human head. Our landlords were
an elderly Albanian couple who moved

slowly and spoke incoherently, as my
Polish father did, in broken English,

their red and white oilskin tablecloth
always graced with a small white bowl

of sunflower seeds for the enormous
caged parrot, who could swear in

impeccably explicit language. The bird
was menacing but obedient to its owners.

Although any visitor was treated
as a home invader. He would begin

by hissing, then moved into a barrage
of curses. The Albanians winnowed

the seeds from their crop after
deadheading the flowers, their kitchen

table having become a staging area
for putting up kernels. After the harvest,

deep in October, the plots
where the sunflowers loomed became

desolate with dried stalks the wind
blew through, with a sound whose tone

underscored the sereness of autumn.
I looked at the stark rows from

the glassed-in porch upstairs, where
I had been stung by a wasp, which made

my finger throb as if it had been hit
by a hammer, but the memory

of the glory of the sunflowers in bloom
continued to fill me, as do the rays

of sunlight that shined into the rooms
of that tawdry railroad flat, bearing its

curled and cracked linoleum, with
a sadness that still pervades me when

I think of awakening there, and hearing
the winds of loss blowing every morning.

Prayer for Yoram Raanan

after Raanan Studio Tour Panorama, June 2013

One views your impressionistic paintings
as one walks through the great halls of our spirit,
the columns of the practice of belief
lining the myriad mirrored visage

of our own colorful becoming and being.
Who enters your painting accesses their soul,
such iconic burning candelabra,
the holographic dove of peace, hovering,

providing resistance against reprisals for all of us.
What inspiration for us to choose
whether we may take retribution or not
before we follow the hallway with many

doors leading to our own tomb,
but it is in your reproducing
those crystalline goblets in oil,
that fills us with so much light,

at least as much as they hold
and allow to pass through so much so
that they chime with their own
illumination, which then intones our own.

How you gild sacred tincture to
the illustrated boards of a book of scriptures.
May the lights of your lavish Menorahs
burn within us for all of our days.

May their twinkling candles
always illumine our darkest hours,
as does the plentitude of luminous schools of
fish you have painted swim through

the inviolate blue of the ocean you envisioned.
How can we ever walk away
without forever being augmented after
viewing your painting of Esther, emerald queen

of deliverance from injustice,
suggestive of the irradiated mystical
painting of Gustave Moreau,
eliciting spiritual luster among the heavier elements,

not without flecks of gold reminiscent of
the illuminated fish of Paul Klee,
but it is the painting of the resilient soul, our true self,
portrayed as crystal arc in human form,

who is bolstered upon blue rays of light
in bright bands which lifts us up
in our own leap of exuberance,
in ever discovering the delight within, the joy without.

The perpetual transcendent not merely
emblematic, but alive, resurrecting itself
out of the flames that ravaged two thousand
of your paintings, whose fiery ash

sparked up amid the devastation among
the forest only to see you rise up, along with us,
to paint the light again in broad strokes
upon which there shines a path through the shadows.

The Day after the 2016 Election

for Art Beck

A dark day in American history, this election
and its results. The old Chinese philosopher
of my imaginative self proclaims,

"String a rope bridge over a windy gorge,
and the rope unravels when enough weight
is placed on it. What is unreliable is strung

like a flimsy rope bridge over a windy gorge,
or a crooked politician elected by a fickle
populace. Woe to the populace. Woe to

those who attempt to traverse the swaying
rope bridge over the windy gorge."
Carl Jung might have said we have lost

touch with our anima and animus, that
we no longer have any concept of what
our mythologies may be. I read your

translation of "The First Duino Elegy."
How many times have I read this, how
many times do I always see something

different in it? Although every time I love
the image of the angels walking among us,
not knowing which of us is dead or alive.

The violin of Rilkean sadness and
melancholy balances with the counterpoint
of the numinous, which intoxicates us,

transfixes us. We are all looking through
the opening of a dark tunnel, and there is
no light to be seen to indicate how far

its end might be. May we all gather enough
strength to kindle within ourselves to find
our way. The next four years will be tortuous,

and as arduous as they might be, may we
cultivate *Bon courage*, as Rodin declared to
Rilke once when he wished him goodnight.

Meeting Amichai

Irene, my co-worker, knew
how much I had revered his poetry,

and when I answered the intercom
downstairs at the bookstore, where

I was busy with a project, all that
she coyly said was, *I think there is*

someone here to see you. Upon
emerging from the basement stairs,

I recognized the visage of his face
immediately, but what I didn't

expect was the warmth of his smile,
the blush that swept across his cheeks

and forehead, the light shining from
his bald pate, as if he had been

illumined by the Palestinian sun
and the lines of his verse became

imbued with that light. We shook
hands, and he offered that he was

reading at the university, but that
it was hush-hush, that the audience

was largely graduate students and
faculty, that he would be traveling to

Berkeley and reading in the Bay Area,
which led us to discuss bookstores,

how well-stocked Cody's Books was.
I was stunned that he wished me well

with my own writing, and I recall
regretting I hadn't something that was

accomplished enough I could show
to him. His humility reechoes

for me these decades later as do
the notes of an oboe, lingering like

an image from his poem, "A Dog
after Love," in which the animal

of his passion is commanded to fetch
his lover's stockings and return

with them between its teeth. Now,
approaching his age, I also recognize

his courage in representing both life
and love in such no uncertain terms,

how having loved and being alone
afterwards are one in the same, only

just a part of the same humming
continuum, as are numinous bands

of sunlight glowing through a maple's
red and orange leaves, and then

the next time I look the backlighting
has receded, allowing us to recognize

how it is that the wonder in living life
is not commensurately just enough but

— in relation to its magnitude —
exponentially so much more than that.

Something Worth Aspiring To

What is worth noting is how
the former Detective Chief Superintendent Foyle

spots the portrait of Samantha Stewart
that her former employer, the artist Sir Leonard

Spencer-Jones, suggested she pose for naked;
and how Foyle, in his inimitable way, wry

facial expression with the lips and mouth, ever
so gingerly draws a silk scarf with a quick pass

of a hand across the portrait of the nude, breasts
and their aureoles fully exposed. Foyle proposes

that Samantha accompany him to London
to a safe house for White Russians, and imparts

that he will drive her, which is a change, since
she had driven him through all the years

of the war; but it is in his drawing the scarf
in folds over the painting, evincing not only

Samantha's nakedness, but also the plain
bareness of her vulnerability, which is nearly

shocking to him, and to us, especially after her
attempt to articulate why she believed she gave

in to Sir Leonard's request that she pose for him
in the first place, with such apparent

embarrassment, we are touched ever so profoundly
that Foyle, the man, would be quite sensitive

to protecting his longstanding friend, whom
he has downplayed his treating as a daughter,

and for us to take away from that
both an active understanding and tenderness,

an insightful discernment of high moral value,
a tacit sense of integrity, a source of guidance

we might steer by, all, and any, of which
would also be something worth aspiring to.

Thirteen Ways of Remembering Lonnie Black

1

An untied silk scarf, a loosened
GQ ascot, adding just that extra
fashionable touch, not so much
flamboyant as the cool suave
that allowed him grace and ease.

2

Parking spaces in Hartford are more
an invention of the imagination than
anything actual; but always artful, no
one can parallel park a car better than
he can, hairsbreadth of inches to spare.

3

What gallery reception can triumph without
him, with his inimitable conception of each
painting gracing the walls, holding his signature
glass of white wine, to which he would add a
strawberry, with his characteristic urbane flourish.

4

What is numerous are the innumerable
breakfasts sitting in a booth over a blue
Formica table at Mo's Downtown, our
conversation always more paramount than
all the home fries he wound up taking home.

5

What venue in Hartford is not now forever
colder by his no longer crossing the threshold
to enliven its ambiance with his presence;
he could have been the mayor, having been
enabled to govern with just a nod, a smile.

6

Those were the times, the peerless early
summer evenings in the Garden, whose idea
he was one of the first to champion; how one
would turn around, suddenly, his mustache
brushing your upper lip, as he lightly kissed you

7

He was his own version of Mr. Rogers in a
classroom of children, he was even referred
to as *The Poetry Man*; seed bags of words
slung over each shoulder, what he planted
took root, burgeoning in young minds.

8

Always in attendance of a friend in need,
willing to listen, offering balm by the salve
of a receptive ear, open heart, he may have
aspired to offering guidance, but he always
endowed dignity to healing, to going on.

9

Advocate *extraordinaire*, writers he knew
may have doubted in their new work, but
his voice quietly beguiled them, nearly in an
assuaging whisper, more blithe than brazen,
can you not hear him say, *Just read your poems.*

10

We can only recollect and wonder if you may
have ever walked with him in Elizabeth Park,
among the trellises of roses, with him stepping
lightly between rows, why each rose clamored to
be the one he may have chosen for his buttonhole.

11
In the gray dawn light of empty Hartford
streets, there appears two wisps drifting silently
over the lawns and the concrete. Ghosts now,
Wallace Stevens and Lonnie Black, precipitating
the blackbirds, one by one, in each tree into flight.

12
Without a book of his own but beloved by many,
he releases his poems for all of us to see —
he helped this person in trouble, comforted
another in a time of need, all of his good deeds now
avid and vivid, like the blackbirds visible all morning.

13
We remember him for many things, well beyond these,
but if you think of him and desire his companionship again,
just walk out into the sunlight; he'll be there in the warmth
on your back, and don't be surprised if blackbirds begin to
flock round what is an angelic presence hovering in air.

The Rain in October

The rain all night, lifting by morning, suffusing the gray
light with silver, and tinting my recollections of other years,
wanting to pry behind what it is that was relevant then
as it is pertinent now, the calling within all of that, the rain
beginning again, lightly, the glistening in that and what is
just beneath that which is what causes me to pause, looking
out at the meadow of Queen-Anne's lace browning to umber,
becoming itself its own sepia photograph, and my walking
back in the misting rain, marveling at just this, this moment
of this day, this rolling of drops of rain across the leaves of
honeysuckle in the windbreak, the bittersweet's beaded
yellow berries, the gilded ochre inflorescence of goldenrod,
the vibrancy even in the waning of that moment becoming
another, rising mist dissolving over the pasture across
the road, the acrid odor of wood smoke, the astonishment in
a candelabra of rain glittering in the pink hydrangea's late bloom.

New Paint on Worn Walls

I feel your pain from afar.
Breach of trust on any level is hard to bear,

but that breach between intimates is unbearable
and the inner tumult that it leads to is disarming

and destructive to one's heart, body, and soul.
As much as you may feel that you will never

trust anyone else again, you more than likely
will, at some point. And that individual will

earn their worthiness of your trust. Your arc
of healing may be quicker than most because

you are going about particulars in a rather
cogent and scrupulous manner. It took

considerable courage for you to confront
your wife's lover. I would imagine that was

freeing to a large extent. Simple things carry
such weight during trying times such as these:

groceries, bike rides, applying new paint
on worn walls. The newness is acting as

a kind of forgetting so you can remember
what it is like to feel alive and at peace again.

Process in times like this appears to exhibit
a protracted sense of drag to you

and the world around you, but process speeds
up when you least expect it and brings you

round again to a new sense of health, slowly,
incrementally, and although

you may not be aware of it you are brought
round again to a fresh resolve,

a restored way of seeing. It happens. It will
happen more often. You will heal.

Present Time

I knock at the door of Gordon King,
retired arborist, of Leverett, and

his wife, Frances, goes to get him,
but before she does so she tells me

he is now blind, and I nod,
then lower my eyes because I had

already known this, grateful for
their kindness, while I wait on

the stone stoop. When he comes to
the door, he points to where the road

will lead me to the cutoff that I need
to go left on, marked by the shagbark

hickory he says I can't miss
by the roadside, where his stand

of trees is more than a mile down
the rutted hardpack. When I stop

the car in front of the small covered
footbridge over the brook, my

yellow Labrador senses the depth
of how special this foray into deep

woods is. She is frisky and romps
between the rows of spruce, as

I judge each one, a saw in hand,
that I took from among the ones

hung on nails on planks on the wall
of the footbridge. When I begin

to cut at the base of the tree I think
best will fill the cathedral ceiling

of the apartment in the refurbished
barn, I inhale the sweet scent of

disturbed leaf litter and pine resin.
The light through the December

woods is a mixture of silver and
gold, glinting through branches

of the leafless trunks of ash and
poplar, the yellowed needles

of tamarack, the green of hemlocks
catching the sun-glint which

they flash in the wind. I will,
drive back down the dirt track

to the main road, with my dog,
and go back to the barn, where

I will place the tree in a stand,
dress the branches in strings of

hundreds of white lights, but for
this instant this is the center

I have and will always experience
knowing, this shining glen beside

the gleam of a sparkling brook,
where nothing but the wind

rushing through the crisp rattle
of leaves increases the quiet;

where when I close my eyes,
momentarily, I can see the sun

through my eyelids, and feel
myself breathing in the moment,

as this morning's wind passes
through the two stalwart maples

beside another barn in another
place, some other year—

there being no time at all between
that one instant and this present time.

Brook Run

My yellow Labrador and I
　　would cross two meadows, separated
　　　　by a tree break and a bridge over

a culvert to the head of the trail
　　through a grove of staghorn
　　　　sumac, where it would wend along

the banks of Cushman Brook.
　　We could leap the small secondary
　　　　rill that fed a sizeable plunge pool

where Cider would swim, fetch
　　the prized pine sticks that
　　　　I brought. One March morning,

the brook running fast with spring rain,
　　she caught a surge of the current
　　　　and rode the stream of it, bobbing,

a few hundred feet down to where
　　she was able to climb back out, tail
　　　　wagging, her legs punctuating

her joy of the ride by high-stepping
　　down the trail, as I ran up to her,
　　　　and she dropped her stick, looking

up at me to indicate that she wanted
　　me to throw it back in so that she
　　　　could ride the current all over again.

All the while thinking I had lost
　　my dog and how irresponsible
　　　　I was in even allowing her to

immerse herself into the quick-
　　ness of the rush of the brook
　　　　after the spring melt. One year,

as we followed the path, with her
   somewhat ahead of me, she halted,
      abruptly, lifting her head to smell

the air, and she turned around to
   return, stopping to look back to me,
      then beginning again, and since

this was unusual for her to do this,
   I followed her back down, over
      the rill, and through the sumac

grove, her pace more of a jog
   than a full run, traversing the far
      meadow, and then the next, home

to the apartment in the barn
   in which we lived; whereupon,
      I picked up the binoculars from

the shelf of the white wooden rack
   by the door, and focused them on
      the trailhead of the path to view

the recognizable head and ears
   of the head of a bear framed among
      sumac leaves; unable to believe

my eyes, putting down the binoculars
   and lifting them again to refocus
      on the space between the trees,

only to notice the black-furred head
   this time had vanished inexplicably,
      as it had appeared, and was gone.

Gathering Sweetness

I spoke with the large kind man
who regularly arranges the produce at Atkins

and mentioned how much I delight in
the native blueberries, as he was unpacking

green cardboard pints of them onto a counter.
What do you use them for, he asked.

My answer was that I ate them for breakfast
every summer morning, with strawberries,

yogurt, and honey. *Oh*, he said, *we'll be
seeing the last of these by next week*,

as I gathered a pint to place into my shopping
basket. This morning, as I was washing

the fruit and placing it into a bowl, topping it
with Greek yogurt, and drizzling it with local

honey, from the farmer, who has named
his land, *Small Ones Farm*, on Bay Road, who

has a modest orchard, and, behind that, hives
of bees, I looked down at my ritual breakfast

with gratitude, knowing, as I do, that I have
only one more serving remaining, that these

are the very last days of August,
that the lushness of summer is thinning into

wizened furrows and brambles of oblivion,
that we move on even when the bloom is

over, the ripeness past, the end in sight.
However, what is only coming to a close,

for this summer, at least, are the native
blueberries and strawberries, and not

the honeybees, all of those little sisters plying
their wings, the ones who we haven't yet

poisoned ourselves with neonicotinoids,
gathering sweetness in the fields of the Lord.

The Enchanted Tailor

— for Fikriye King

You mend my old khakis; tear out
    the shredded lining of black silk
        in my Yale Genton frock coat,

replace it with a new one,
    quoting what price it would
        normally cost, and what you

will charge me, which is half
    off. You ask me if there is
        an extra for the one missing

button that fell off below
    the collar of a favorite green
        summer shirt, and after looking

along the front tail, where
    some are often sewn, I am
        embarrassed to say there isn't;

and you lightly reprimand me
    as if I were a relative, of which
        I am honored to be if I could,

but you suggest that you will
    find two black emerald buttons
        of for replacements, snip off

the single lonesome one, and sew
    them both on, so I can then affix
        them to my button-down collar.

When I pick up the shirt
    later in the week, you ask me,
        How you like, and I answer you

with an appreciative nod
    and my smile, asking, *How much.*
        You answer, *Two dollars*, and

we bask in the glow of what is
    good company, your Radio Free
        Europe/Radio Liberty station

broadcasting news in Turkish;
    a friend of yours from your
        Muslim prayer group, laughing

delightedly over the decorative
    embellishments you have woven
        into what may be a festivity of

wedding dresses assembled
    together on a line in your shop,
        beside a poster for an event in

town to raise funds for
    the refugees from the war in Syria.
        I pay you for making my old

shirt new again, and in what is
    only a passing moment another
        business transaction of ours is

over again, until I find another
    tear in yet one more seam,
        or discover wear in my paisley

comforter which has warmed me
    for many winters, that you find
        a way to tuck up, to stitch over,

to renew any wear or frays with
    needle and thread, unwinding from
        what appears to be your magical

spool, from which you are able to
    repair what are endless imperfections
        in the clothes we wear and what

we might keep bundled
    around us to stem the unremitting
        bitterness of being underdressed

in the cold, which has no
    borders, knowing that, as you do,
        the fabric of lovingkindness fits all.

Sunnyside-up in a Blanket

Singing with simplicity may
    just make for an elegant song that
        flourishes with the clearest notes.

This morning's goldfinch in the kousa
    dogwood is imploring us all to listen
        to how *sweet* the new day is, what it

is for exactly what it is, without even
    considering the possibilities of what
        it holds. While savoring the wisdom

of the goldfinch, I crack an egg into
    hot olive oil, cover the small skillet
        with a glass top, so I can watch how

the egg progresses in solidifying its
    white and yolk, while the cinnamon-
        raisin English muffin is in the toaster.

When the egg is nearly done, I place
    a couple of slices of brie onto it, and
        then turn the heat down to low, so it

can melt without drying out the yolk.
    This is my Sunnyside-up in a blanket,
        simplicity lavished in a little *coloratura*,

the day's clear notes of inspiration,
    my nourishment of aesthetics and
        protein, which for whatever reason

precipitates the recollection of when
    I was a child, and my overly-stern
        father relinquished, after the death

of my mother, to allow me to wear
    the Zorro costume for Halloween,
        little asthmatic that I was; and how

I couldn't breathe well with the mask
    on, due to the smell of the painted
        plastic, but how I was determined to

be Zorro for a night; and when
    I removed the mask, my face blotched
        with hives, I was all that more lonelier

than before, inexplicitly bringing me
    closer to my essence, which is
        what has occurred this morning,

brought on by my friend the goldfinch
    and his song, and my recipe of
        a simple egg wrapped in brie, served

with buttered toast, smothered
    with blueberry preserve, which unlike
        my childhood experience as Zorro,

has, in savoring every bite,
    brought me closer to my true essence,
        unmasking my brighter side and yours.

The Word

after Pathwork Lecture, No. 233,
"The Power of the Word," *channeled by*
Eva Pierrakos, September 25, 1975

The word is the sum total
of what you believe, whatever

it is that you are; it carries the tone
of whatever ethos you exhibit,

what colors expand in your aura,
the arrangement of what planets

orbit around any sun, or whether
or not there is one exercising

the draw of its gravitational force.
The word is the master switch,

the soul's lever, what illuminates
the flash of the spirit,

what energizes cosmic design.
The word expands within the dust

of the brushstrokes from God's
hand to Adam's in Michelangelo's

ceiling of the Sistine Chapel;
its images shimmer in the vibrant

combination of pastels in the oils
of a painting by Seurat, in which,

as he intended, we discover
harmony in emotion; it emanates

from the perpetuity in not only
the slant but also in the fragrance

of the falling of autumn rain
carved in Hiroshige's woodblocks.

The Hallway

I awakened between my mother, who had fallen
asleep with me after the late movie, with the theme

music, I would later learn, from Leroy Anderson's
The Syncopated Clock, and my father, home from

the factory and second shift at Pratt & Whitney.
I awakened to the soliloquy coming from the hallway

leading to my grandmother's room, which already
bore its mystery, with the grates of the heat register

that resembled an installation from another world,
especially when it ticked during a cold Floridian

winter night. I would sidle out over the covers
between my parents to the bottom edge of the bed,

slide off, and then toddle toward the doorway where
I remember my grandmother motioning and speaking

passionately to what I was convinced I saw as a cold
translucent mist which apparently, to my wide eyes,

floated there before her. Grandmother's muffled
sobbing and unabashed keening was all rather

hair-raising to a five-year-old, who was so bewitched
by the display, I was willing to risk walking

in the darkness of the hallway, the flashlight in one
of my grandmother's hands beaming its ray at me.

What she explained to me the next morning was that
this was what became of my grandfather, in whose

strong but gentle voice I found solace in a household
of perpetual histrionics, at a dining room table where

I looked for the American food my friends were served
to feast on in what seemed to be perpetual abundance.

Although, instead of hamburgers, hot dogs, and the prize
dessert of the 1950's, jello, made from a mold, we had

pig's feet in gelatin, smelts, beet borscht, and sauerkraut
with kielbasa. The nightly theatrics of my grandmother,

dramatized in her black housecoat, with the small faded
sad roses, speaking to my grandfather's ghost, has also

remained with me until I am now the age my grandmother
was. My dead grandfather and I making our occult

pilgrimages, separately, in the hallway, and my not quite
understanding what I saw or what I thought I had seen;

but remembering my mouth being agog, as I trundled
back to bed, under the stern direction of my parents'

perturbed voices issuing from the bedroom, and knowing,
in later years, that this was all about the love

my grandmother and my grandfather had for each other —
with her always scolding him for leaving her alone in this

world, to which he responded by reappearing to her in their
nighttime hallway trysts, as often as she might desire.

The Swist

The Swist is a brook. As child, the name
was often intentionally

mispronounced by classmates who would
also insert the word cheese after rending

the air with hyperbole. As a grown man,
particularly women, on a date, would

rhyme Swist with Twist, and then say, *Just
like Chubby Checker, right?* Often enough,

I have needed to have to speak each
letter of it over the phone to a Customer

Service Representative, enunciating
the letters twice; only to hear, *Yes, Swift,*

repeated back to me, the consternation
rising in my pulse and shooting right

through the top of my head; my ire
surfacing through my repetition, once

again, of the four consonants protecting
that one vowel in the middle, with

the sinuousness of the soft consonants
providing a rush until the final hard sound,

as in following a straightaway before
a sudden meander. The Swist rises in

Rhineland-Palatinate at 330 meters
above sea level on the Eifel. The brook

is nearly 44 kilometers long, and in
North Rhine-Westphalia it joins the mouth

of the Erft. The Swist flows through
my veins, as readily as it tumbles into

Swisttal, a municipality; and its rush
may be heard in Meckenheim and

Flerzheim, which is considered to be
a berg of the town Rheinbach. It is here

that there are cycle paths along
the edge of the brook, where lovers lie

in the grass and children play among
wildflowers. The Swist also gives

its name to the town of Weilerswist.
The source of my namesake is

found at the northern edge of the Eifel.
Considered to be the longest brook

run in Europe, the Swist may explain
why I find healing in moving water.

from

The Bees of the Invisible

(2019)

A Wild Beauty

Every poem is a momentary stay against
the confusion of the world.
Robert Frost

To salvage the last
of the heirloom roses
after the morning rain,
to place them in
a clear crystal vase
without water,
so that I may dry

the florets
and remaining petals,
to preserve
their sweet fragrance,
to nourish
ourselves against
heartache. The snipped

wild red roses
drying in their vase
are prayers imploring us
to look within
to find the flame
flickering with such
a wild beauty

that it extinguishes
the smothering darkness.
Salvaging the last roses
this morning in the rain,
my body awoke to
the coolness, to a scent
that exhilarates, which, if

we can preserve it,
nurtures us through what
are calculated avaricious
rants, vortices of disorder,
with what serves us
as an uncanny sustenance,
its own inexplicable elixir.

Evanescence

What is peripheral is
     often not even what is considered,
          but what passes just beyond
               our vision may momentarily

flutter there and be so enchanting
     that it offers a revelation as to
          why butterflies are emblematic
               of the evanescent. That black-

winged spicebush swallowtail, as
     large as a hand, takes my breath
          away, in flight among hydrangea
               and wild mint, appearing then

disappearing as quickly as it flies
     into view; and this species differs
          from the tiger swallowtail, which
               is infused with yellows that recall

summer dawn, with vestiges of
     the inky traceries of the midnight sky.
          However, it is the Puckish dances
               of the relatively small inhabitants

of the butterfly world that charm
     and mollify the most intemperate
          mood, such as the brilliant yellow-
               green of the clouded sulphurs;

the orange-gray of the coppers;
     what appears to be only the color-
          less pale wings of the cabbage
               whites, that on second look reveals

a black eye-spot on each wing.
Then there are the blue azures that
fly up when you are stepping
through the tall summer grass;

and the lacey brown-orange
winged elfins, who flit moth-like
but revel in the copses along
dusty roadsides. The inordinate

surprise of silver-bordered
fritillaries pausing among reeds
of an inland pond never ceases to
provide the marvel of their fanning

those wings of pure orange,
with their Rorschach of black dots;
but here and there we may be
spellbound by a checkerspot's

primal colored harmony of orange,
white, and brown; or the admiral's
intrinsic parentheses of either
red and brown or white and blue-

black; the red-spotted purple's lush
indigo as it spreads light blue bands
caught in a gust among an opening
of windy meadow grass; what is

diminutive in comparison with its
larger cousin, the viceroy's orange
and black, as it finds shade among
the willows and aspens, is not to be

confused with the monarch, which
    is larger and whose orange is muted,
        and with wings always held at an angle,
            as it glides from one nourishing pod

of milkweed to another, to fortify
    itself for the immense journey south
        where it migrates to overwinter
            in firs in the mountains of Mexico.

September Morning

Sky clear after rain,
alleviating six weeks of drought;
sunny, with a hint of coolness
in the shadows beside the barn

and under the trees, speckled
with a fringe of fleabane;
the orb weaver web on the porch,
sticky with spiral capture silk,

containing another victim —
a praying mantis wrapped in
a winding sheet; and
the Queens-Anne's lace bending

in the meadow under the weight
of a heavy dew.

Confluence

August morning, sunlight
    flickering through
        green canopy of birch,

tulip trees, white pine.
    Step by step
        in rhythm, even at

the steep incline
    after the falls,
        where the brook spills

into her first pools.
    Suddenly, the triangular
        head, the stout body,

weaving through
    speckled leaf litter,
        undulating at my pace.

I raise one leg,
    she passes underneath —
        then the other,

we two
    in harmony with
        a divine cadence. I turn

my head in astonishment.
    She slithers toward
        the trout lilies brightening

the edge of the brook.
    She looks at me
        as she wriggles beneath

my scissor kick. Is it awe?
    She slips into
        the sunlight warming

the stones above the rush
    of water, flicks her
        tongue, pauses to drink.

From the fire tower
    at the summit of the mountain,
        I can see the whole valley

Ode to Jack LaLanne

Charles Atlas had nothing on you.
Those of us who knew of
the muscle-bound boys who kicked

sand in our face at the beach
weren't of the same caliber,
nor of a similar inner substance

as you, who would never even think
of stepping down from your firm
moral fiber, as steely as the muscles

you exercised to build. Only a bully
such as Donald Trump would be
attracted to the mindless authority

of kicking sand into people's faces,
only a true weakling would
even consider something so reviled.

You were a boyhood hero,
and I think of you every morning now,
as an old man, when I raise the shades,

to begin my own daily routines —
my three laps at the mall. Even before
our fathers rose from their sleep

from the late shift, or were
on their way out the door for the first,
you had already slipped on your wet

suit, and were pulling a tugboat in
New York harbor, stroking through
the cold currents of the Hudson River;

or doing over a thousand pushups in
only a matter of some twenty minutes;
or shackled with chains, swimming

from Alcatraz to San Francisco,
police following in a boat just to keep
sharks, just twenty feet from you, away.

Children, who were still in pajamas,
lucky enough to be watching your
15-minute morning exercise program,

were in awe of you and your brand,
of your proving yourself, and the risks
you took. You showed us how to love

ourselves, to nurture our bodies, but
you also inspired us by writing books,
acquiring a doctorate in exercise science.

I still think of you every morning, Jack
LaLanne, every time I raise the shades,
each time I complete a lap at the mall;

you who lived to be 96, who espoused
the Greek ideal; who, even if you had
the chance, and we are sure that you did,

would have deferred, would have walked
away from any opportunity of kicking
sand in someone's face, especially that

of Charles Atlas; and you would have
been someone who would have stood up
to the insolence of Donald Trump.

The Space Between

for Christine Cote

There's a lot to be said
for being able to appreciate
the uncertain space between
winter and spring, an unusually long space
this year, after an unending winter.

Easy enough to mention
finding wood anemone, bluets, trout lily,
and violets. What is radiant draws us,
holds our attention, replenishes
our hope in the seeds

of regeneration springing into flower. This
serves us. As does Nadezdha Mandelstam
in *Hope Against Hope*, when she gives back
the egg her husband, Osip,
had begged from neighbors for her supper

before he was arrested under orders
by Stalin and taken to be imprisoned
in the Gulag. Being grateful
to witness the space
between winter and spring is a grace

few of us fully fathom, that grayness between
the melting ice and snow
and the brittle emptiness of the leaf litter
beneath the budless trees. This may resemble
the truth we seek more than the hope

we gird ourselves with to staunch
the ruthlessness of an authoritarian regime,
intolerant of compassion
or a cognizance of what is moral.
The space between may prove to be

a meditative and more prudent path to take
between the grayness of one season
and the animation of another,
before we are truly surprised by
an indescribable joy upon seeing

the ineffable yellows spangled by the lily
and the speckled whites of anemone that
mark the distance between winter and spring.
There's a lot to be said
about oppression and freedom,

between our seeking truth
and the abundant hope found
in the young black snake's sinuousness
sliding between the first wildflowers,
or a cotillion of box turtles sunning on a log.

Release

1   To be on,
        for it to be one of your better days,
        for it to culminate
        in knowing, beyond a doubt,
        that placing your hands in the air
        just at the right moment,
        so that you can bring them together
        and softly palm
        the trapped sparrow flying around
        the bookstore café
        is to experience a moment
        of the marvelous, then to step
        outside to open your hands
        to release the bird
        and to watch it fly up
        over the languishing blossoms
        of the hanging cherry tree,
        is to also release that
        wilderness within yourself
        back into the open air.

2   Seeing whatever it was
        that had darted in front of your eyes
        out of the barnyard at dusk
        reminds you of the bat
        in the auditorium at the book signing
        that flew up above the heads
        of the onlookers during a break,
        then dodged coffee urns
        and fruit Danish while
        knocking over stacks of paper coffee cups
        before you could pull off a tablecloth
        from a free table,

and corner the bat, urging it through
a series of hallways that led to a storeroom,
where you threw the red cloth into
the air, and the bat flew into it,
as it landed onto the checkered
linoleum floor. Kneeling down
to bunch the cloth loosely about
the bat, you could feel the nervous
twitching of its wings
beneath the fiber of the cotton
weave, and walked it outside,
where you tossed the tablecloth up
to release the bat
in the falling rain, upon which
it chose to attach itself
to the crenellated concrete
of the outside wall of the building,
blinking its eyes in the freedom
of a new day, adjusting
its sight to everything, all of which
appeared to be nothing less than remarkable.

Dominic Savio

I perceived your sweetness from your haloed portrait
on the prayer card. The Jesuits in charge of our parish
created an after school club dedicated in your name.

To be aligned with you meant that we might have
a calling; after all, we were eager to hear angelic voices,
and the small white missals we read from, and carried

into Mass, were fragrant with candles and holy water.
The gilt edges of the book sent a shiver in me every time
I rubbed my index finger along the glimmer I thought

might have emanated from you. Our vestments, such
as the white surplice we wore, resembled those of altar
boys, although we had red sashes to adorn our slender

waists, making us look like a host of prepubescent martyrs.
Dominic Savio, student of Saint John Bosco, who died
of pleurisy at 14, you were canonized for your *heroic virtue*.

Your last words to your father were that you had already
forgotten what the parish priest had taught you, but,
oh, what wonderful things you were just beginning to see.

Hawk Feathers

Mid-February snowmelt mud,
the field's expanse;

at the southern edge, a porcupine
barks and bristles, edges away

into a clutch of winterberry.
Hemlock forest, the blight

of wooly adelgid, green club moss,
browned bracken along the border.

Beyond, the trail winds through trees;
blowing mist spreads through branches.

Here, hawk feathers litter the ground:
one cluster, then another . . .

Bending down in the drizzle,
I gather one feather, yet another,

and another, as if reaching
each time for an answer.

Remembering Ruth Stone

After reading *In the Next Galaxy*,
I phoned Ruth Stone, who was living in her home
in Johnson, Vermont.
I wanted her to read for a small honorarium.

"I am blind," she said. "I just can't do it,
but I would have liked to do it.
Thank you for asking me and for knowing
about my work."

I even offered to drive up
to Vermont, put her up in the campus hotel,
and drive her back from the reading,
if she wished. But she thought better of it.

I learned that she died shortly thereafter.
She was the real thing: deeply human, astoundingly
beautiful voice, a great but overlooked poet,
who would have almost preferred to remain that way.

I just wanted to get to know her, to listen
to her silences more deeply.
Over the phone her voice sounded like an angel,
trapped in a sightless darkness.

I hope that when she passed over
the veil was lifted from her eyes, how then she could
see the whorl of light she entered *in the next galaxy*,
where she herself became a constellation.

Spring Rain

This stark era of Trump,
and the absurdity America
has become, with the legion

of criminals leading the country,
and the low bar set by their
example that has allowed

the psychic free radicals to run
amok, I think of that moment
of perpetual sweetness in 1961,

when Audrey Hepburn and
George Peppard played out
the last scene in *Breakfast*

at Tiffany's, when they find
the lost cat and stand in an
embrace, with the orange tabby

between them, in the falling rain
on a sidewalk in New York,
while Henry Mancini's orchestra

kicks in with the score of
Moon River, the deluge continuing
to fall; Hepburn and Peppard

steadfastly engaged in an enduring
kiss, memorably soaked to
the skin in their London Fog

trench coats, and a '58 two-tone
blue and white Chevy, with fins,
drives past. The camera, panning

overhead, begins to fade, leaving
Holly Golightly and Paul Varjack
with us, to perpetuate

in the American psyche forever.
To be that wet with rapture,
and drenched in such exhilaration,

inspires me to whistle along
to the tune, knowing that we, oh,
so much want to be that happy, too.

The Vision: Two Sonnets

1   You saw this with eyes closed
    and spoke it to me —
    the image floating there,
    settling itself within your own mind,

    within mine: the tall calla lily
    standing on its green stem
    in all its whiteness; and behind it
    the violet aura we read about,

    from which the Archangel Zadkiel
    embodies spiritual alchemy,
    God's freedom, forgiveness, justice —
    with Saint Germain, whose work

    aligns with the-seat-of-the-soul,
    whose twin flame color is amethyst.

2   You tell me that
    a small, white bundle, which remains
    an inscrutable mystery, is placed deep
    within the trumpet-shaped leaf,

    or spathe, of a calla lily, beside
    its spadix. You tell me that the lily
    takes the little bundle unto its folds,
    that the lily wraps itself around it,

    that this archetypal image fades
    in the glimmering violet aura,
    that after it hovers there, momentarily,
    in the ethereal realm, sacrosanct,

    in sacred space, it enters into perpetuity,
    where it remains, freely opened within us.

The Practiced Silence

Estes Park, 1972

There was hiking the trail eight miles
up to a campsite beside Boulder Brook,

waist-high blonde grasses waving on
either side of the trail, and the next day

feeling lightheaded from the elevation
but just forging ahead to the open

expanse of Grand Lake to fish for perch,
the fragrance of which emanating

from the campfire alerted a ranger
later that evening. This meant walking

down to the trailhead to pay the $50
fine for fishing without a license, and

walking back up, which was alright
if you're 19; but it was returning that

afternoon, and immersing myself by
reading a book on a flat rock in

the middle of the torrent, cleansing me
with its roar; and then the next morning

awakening, clear-eyed, to
the echo hammered by a flicker, who

was debugging the pine bark, and to
the practiced silence of the kit fox,

sniffing the backpack hung on an high
branch of a felled tree that contained

the eggs for breakfast, those black
furred feet quickening into a leap from

along the tree trunk onto the sandy
shore, where it stopped,

momentarily, just to look back at me,
never quite receding from memory,

before trotting away
to enter the shadows beneath the pines.

What We Ever Really Need to Know

All we need to know
is that Magdalene, Mary, the mother
of James, and Salome came
in the darkness before morning to

His tomb to anoint the body with
spices and oils. That alone
is beautiful. Just the thought of
anointing the dead body of Jesus

makes us pause with astonishment —
His body battered and bloodied,
then crucified, the five wounds
from the nails in His hands and feet,

the lance mark near His heart.
All we need to know
is that Joseph of Arimathea removed
Jesus from the cross, wrapped

His body in linen, and placed it in
a tomb, which was cut into rock,
like a cave, that a stone, weighing
possibly as much as two tons, was

lifted into the opening, on grooves,
upon which it could be slid into
place, only by several strong men.
All we need to know

is that Magdalene, Mary, the mother
of James, and Salome found the stone
rolled away, the body of Jesus gone,
an empty pile of bloody linens

in which the body had lain.
All we need to know

is that they were all startled into tears
by the depth of their amazement,

that they probably placed their baskets
of oils and spices on the rocky ground,
that they embraced each other,
that they knew what they knew,

that there was a plenitude and
a providence in the joy of their knowing.
All we need to know
is that as the sun rose out of the darkness

the light entered the cave in the rock,
that as the sun had risen,
so had Christ, that the women could
be seen dancing, their arms raised,

crying out, *Hallelujah*, that as they
danced and sang, what had transpired
from the spiritual alchemy in that cave
was such that His rising up was also

our ascension if we only were so bold
to believe in such a revolutionary act
as our own hearts opening in resurrection
within us, resolutely without question,

opening to Christ consciousness, opening
to *I art thou*, to such an inviolate
unspoken mystery, the whirling
cosmos inside me and you, to awaken to

what is beatific, as was the light
Magdalene, Mary, the mother of James,
and Salome danced in, which
is really all that we ever need to know.

Frittata

It could be the alluring sun after a full day
of rain, bringing out my better nature, or
that making brunch is more of a creative

solution than usual with a refrigerator scant
of leftovers. Choosing the largest
extra-large egg makes for pairing with

remaining scraps of cheese. Selecting
a sweet onion, from the French-blue bowl,
is an aesthetic pleasure in itself, before

I peel and halve it, then cut it thinly into
slices, which take no time to brown
in butter and olive oil, filling the kitchen

with more than just a promise of piquancy.
Pouring the beaten egg into the skillet,
I find my own center, as the mixture fills

its perfect roundness, a circumference
which fills with a brightness that could
not only augur nourishment but happiness.

Though it is the goat cheese and cheddar
that will inflect various tones in taste,
and after distributing these I dust cracked

black pepper and red pepper flakes
over these esteemed contents in the skillet.
Covered, at low heat is best, so it can

coalesce, before it can be plated, sliding,
whole, onto a platter, affixed with buttered
toast points, and accompanied by

a hearty salad bursting with cucumbers
and leafy greens. There it is, awaiting
my fork, steaming in the spring air,

and when I finish, with the medley
of tastes coating my palate, I am filled
with the goodness of the contents

of this circle. Consuming what was
once whole, I am made ready to begin
whatever it is that needs to be done.

Opossum

The number slaughtered on
the road through the swamp
is appalling. Driving

home late in thick fog,
the largest opossum I have
ever seen stepped out over

the double-yellow
line, stopping there
to stare at me, paralyzed by

the car's headlights.
The eerie coals of its eyes
burned in the night, coils

of blowing fog swirled
around the bristling hairs
of its body and the long

spiky tail, accounting for
a third of its body. The garish
moon-white face and dark

eyebrows foreshadowing
the pink wet nose particularly
makes the opossum's face

look nightmarish. Walking
down the hill beside the gate
to Mount Pollux during

a snowstorm, I paused to
listen to what first sounded
like the sibilance of falling

snow, but then turned
toward the tangled wands
of bare cat briar to make

out the gray, black, and white
of an opossum's coat that blended
in with the snowy branches,

realizing that these sounds
I faintly heard issued from
the opossum's open mouth

that it clearly held
in a snarl, brandishing those
storied fifty teeth, more than

any other North American mammal,
besides the Orca and armadillo;
its fierce threat display causing

me to begin to walk slowly
past the lair of this solitary
marsupial, this cranky marsh

and woodland hermit, until
I was out of earshot of its
gnashing of teeth and hissing.

Walt Whitman on Donald Trump

Oh, you snake oil selling *provocateur*,
you faux gilded imposter
selling authoritarianism for American
democracy, may you choke
on your own phlegm-filled speeches,
your conspiratorial rants,
your endless quiver of lies, whose

equivocal insults you brandish
and shoot like arrows
at those whose integrity you should
quaver beneath instead of belittling.
You choose to ruin and impede
instead of build and facilitate. Your
brand of hatred scars

and lacerates, leaving a barren swath
in its wake. You've long ago made
a deal with the devil, and even he has
stepped aside from your burning
wrath and vehemence.
May the best in us topple you
and the ugliness of your kind, may we

persevere in preserving our largesse
and swamp you in the imbecility
of your own making, your smallness
of character, or lack thereof entirely;
the soulless fluke that you are, whose
odious turpitude rages
in the monstrous wake you leave

for the history you will never be able to
rewrite, for the dark legacy
you will come to be known for,
and the spiritual insolvency with which
you have defrauded all of the people.
May the echoes of your offensive
and irritating pseudo-flamboyance ring

in your own ears. May your defiant
windup toy impressions
of how and what eloquent presidents
walk and talk like
strike you down in your spitefulness.
May you crawl like the worm that
you are. May we reinhabit the earth.

The Bees of the Invisible

We wildly gather the honey of the invisible in order
to store it in the great golden hive of the invisible.
Rainer Maria Rilke, *from* The Poet's Guide to Life:
The Wisdom of Rilke, *translated by Ulrich Baer*

I recognize a sacredness
in the kousa dogwood this morning
as I have no other
morning, noticing its red fruit
ripening among the branches
that the barnyard squirrel
will gorge on when it is at its peak,

which marks the end of summer
and autumn's incipience.
How difficult it is to give up
August's lushness,
in all of its wildness,
to the glorious diminishment
of September, with its flashy golden

days, the mornings drenched
with heavy dew, each one surprising
as purple asters appearing
amid the cool shadows of the grass.
In winter, when the snow accrues
the rabbits that burrow
in the juniper hedge emerge

to nibble the bark of the dogwood
since they are unable to browse,
and they strip a few inches from
the base of the tree; but now
I am drawn to the counterpoint
of the catbird's cry
and the throbbing pulse of cicadas.

In making things whole,
the bees of the invisible hover
above deep blue stands of chicory
lingering amid the flat tops
of Queen Anne's lace that flourish
among the leaning swaths
of timothy's newly gilt inflorescence.

Three Poems: The Talcott Arboretum

1 *Pandan*

We sit on a green
    wooden bench in
        the Talcott Arboretum at Mount Holyoke,

opposite the subtropical
    Pandanus, whose family is also known
        as *screw pine*, an ancient food source used

since the mid-
    Cretaceous. Its inflorescences are
        spiked umbels, or terminally-borne racemes,

whose brightly colored
    subtended spathes were nowhere
        to be seen on this winter day, the snow falling

beyond the greenhouse
    windows. We sit in bliss,
        holding hands, meditating together on the wild

extravagance of the green
    sheaves, of how the *Pandanus utilus*
        might be compared to the hubbub of a lavish

haute cuisine dinner party or,
    more apt, the fourth chakra, our
        heart-center, pleasure supreme, consummated

sensual love.
    The Pandan is so lush that even
        in death it is beautiful: the tips of its serrated

sword-like leaves
    turn from an aesthetic
        translucent yellow to a handsome herbal brown.

The Pandan's infectious
    lushness instills a sense
        of joy, fills us with a spiritual radiance, warming us

in our inner ascendency,
    alerting us that what is beyond is something
        more than just the noon sun haloed by snow clouds.

2. *Cattlianthe*

What greets you in the greenhouse
    is what is perhaps the most
        resplendent shade of purple orchid,

intergeneric genus of Chiapas,
    Belize, Guatemala, and Honduras,
        Cattilianthe Orchidaceae, that

is related to the Chocolate Drop,
    who is named after its white-tipped
        deep red petals, *Volcano Queen*;

and the Cattlianthe Jewel Box,
    whose pure red is called *Scherazade* —
        and what stories it must have to tell.

Cattlianthe, you announce yourself
    as does the color priests wear during
        Eastertide to ascribe devotion

to the *Passion*; or those women
    elders, who wear this color
        to announce their coming of age,

exponentially, to their beauty
    in wisdom. The fragrance of this
        orchid is sublime, a divine mist

of scent, which invokes the memory
    of your lover, nonpareil, exquisite,
        unlike any other, in a room that is lit

by mirrors, reflecting sky, whose
    passages are filled with sunlight and
        the migrations of flocks of birds.

3 *Anthurium*

You are nearly lost beneath
    the tall flowers of Illium floridanum,
        known as Star-Anise, or Stink Bush:

first, because of its sweetly fragrant
    leaves; second, due to the fishy smell
        of its nearly imperceptible, or hidden,

small red florets. The juxtaposition
    is fitting, somehow, since you are
        known for your consummate flowers —

being both male and female, whose
    dense whorls of blossoms are contained
        in a flourish around the prong of your

spadix, held in the air. Your nickname
is Manua Kea White, and there is
a speckled splash of red at the center

of your blooms, which constellates
across their textured whiteness,
spangled as the specks of a galaxy

spread out across each petal's
creamy expanse. When we stand
next to you, we can't help but realize,

from your benevolent presence, that
not only are we all part of a whole,
but also that *all* is one.

Ravening

I felt the initial force of it
at 3:00 a.m. when a blast hit the front
of the house, sending the windows
rattling. All morning the winds

carved up swaths of air in the sky.
Their force was Magellanic
in magnitude, since what the winds
blew swept over the land, since

the winds roared while blasting away
the clouds, since the winds scrubbed
the trees free of loose branches, since
whatever wasn't bolted down

was blown, and wreaked, and wasted.
The late February winds
ravaged the landscape and struck down
trees onto homes, as if they were

an extension of the government, a sign
of dystopian devastation, the rolling back
of common sense, environmental policy
run amok, ensuring swaths of barren land.

The late February winds
launched some real howlers, burrowing
through the crowns of trees,
littering the countryside, as does

ignorance and malevolence,
with a savagery of deadfall limbs and,
wherever you look, just like a ravening,
a veritable detritus of little sticks.

Written Upon the Death of W. S. Merwin

Day of windblown cloud,
cold blue shadows crossing over the remaining
patches of snow;

the first green needles
pricking the air in the coiled red branches
of stinging nettles

make me remember
your poem, "Urticophilia,"
your caution to us to hold

the nettles tightly in our hands
so as not to become infected
by the sharp leaf-hairs that inject

irritants into the skin
that cause an irradiated itchiness
which swells the affected epidermis

to the extent
that even just grazing the leaf-hairs
results in an unimaginable tingling,

a red rash that spreads,
that inflames follicles and sets them ablaze,
with nagging discomfort;

and how, instead, in your poem,
you teach us to gather the young leaves
to make a memorable soup.

Hearing the news of your death,
we gather the leaves of your poems,
savor their lines, their elegance,

appreciate their full resonance,
their taste of infinity,
the full flavor of then and now

in their timelessness —
for all ages throughout time
are, and will be, always present:

you who leave us such a legacy of astonishment,
you who have become one with the distant horizon,
you who have now become one of the ancients.

Ley Lines

*An imaginary line between some important places
such as hills, believed to be where there were very old
paths . . . sometimes thought to have special powers.*
Cambridge Dictionary

We walk up
Pine Hill Road in Conway. Saturday afternoon,

early April buds spearing up through the muddy
ground. Nearly twenty years

since we drove up the steep hill that summer
we parked beside the stone wall

of the meadow, just past the Archibald MacLeish
homestead, to picnic in the hayed meadow.

Where we now stand, Mount Monadnock
is seen clearly in the distance, in southern

New Hampshire. Towering stands of pines rock
in the brisk wind. We survey the meadow, after

twenty winters and twenty springs, the alder
grove that has sprung up, the hummocks

and tussocks that provide character
to its bumpy ground. The tangled tall grass

is tawny, before the sunlight greens it
into sheaves, then browns it again, wind-whipped

and leaning, beaten-down in places, where deer
have lain to weather the frigid winter cold.

This is where we found the grace in laying
down a memory, with a straw picnic basket,

containing sandwiches, wine, and fruit; where
we revisit, and experience how that time

still exists, will always be a part of us
and our own mythology, the winds buffeting us.

We embrace, find ourselves in the timelessness
of our lives together, reaching out for each other's

aging hands, touching what it is
that reconnects us to the ley lines of our existence.

Lullaby

If I lose you one day,
will you then sleep alone
without my murmuring beside you,
as do branches of the linden?

Absent of me lying beside you, always
astir and leaving you with my words,
soft as eyelids, across your breasts,
your arms, your mouth.

Minus my being near you,
so you can be alone with who you are,
as in a garden, with clusters
of aromatic mint, the spicy star-anise.

from Maria Rilke's New Poems *(1907)*

Schlaflied

Einmal wenn ich dich verlier,
wirst du schlafen können, ohne
dass ich wie eine Lindenkrone
mich verflüstre über dir?

Ohne dass ich hier wache und
Worte, beinah wie Augenlider,
auf deine Brüste, auf deine Glieder
niederlege, auf deinen Mund.

Ohne dass ich dich verschließ
und dich allein mit Deinem lasse
wie einen Garten mit einer Masse
von Melissen und Stern-Anis.

New Poems

(2020)

Salutations: *after Antonio Porchia*

for Richard Shaw

1
The fields are buttercupped
and edged with ragged robin.

We've entered the realm
of the subtle variegations of the colors of summer.

2
Wishing you well on a mid-June evening,
one on which the fading light of dusk

is struck with nothing less
than what I call an inner splendor spreading outward.

3
Revel in the day. Each moment offers up specific delight:
the thick sweet scent of mulitflora roses; an oriole's bright
call,

repeating itself; Deptford-pink blooming
along the southern windbreak, among yellow tansy.

4
Ah, you have seen the first fireflies,
the fireflies blinking in the darkness,

filling you with their otherwordly light,
marking their appearance, enrapt with wonder.

Green Lake, Ellsworth, Maine

Striated layers of clouds form, dissolve,
reshape over the aqueous mirror

that is Green lake. Their reflections
ripple, pool around rocks, wash

over stones. We sit in the accumulating
darkness infused with sunset,

surrendering ourselves to the subtlety
of dusk suffusing the fir woods. Shoals

of dark purple bands, the shade
of lupines in bloom, blend into a pink

incarnation of the wildflower
gone past above another layer

of cloud, lined with wisps of gold,
of rose, that disappears entirely

into smoke across the silver sky,
until it all gives way to an accord —

the whole horizon opening up
to the rush of stars that fill

the imminent darkness with sparkling
light that reflects the lapping waters,

their ceaseless hush, with such
breathlessness that compels one's mouth

to form in a circle in which to express
the exclamation, *Oh*, as in prayer,

which, when uttered repeatedly,
reiterates the monosyllable of gratitude.

Purple Iris

for Gabriel Rummonds

They bloom above
the yellow dazzle of cosmos
and even after the sticky sweetness
of the vibrant petals of red peonies
were shattered by wind and rain.

These royal purple iris,
reigning atop their thin stems,
announce themselves
as royalty to the garden,
their petals veined with magenta

and tipped at their center
with a dab of yellow,
holding themselves
open, as if always flying upward,
their emanation a similar hue

as that associated with Zadkiel
and the angels of the purple light ray,
whose auras are so memorable
that they appear
as they appear, etched and emblazoned,

by a divine aesthetician,
and providing not just contentment,
which can merely be palpable,
but also constitutes a healing visage,
a balm for the eyes —

as if the irises themselves
are rinsed by their color
pervading the air, and in their
uncommon, but simple, decorum,
avail themselves in cleansing us all.

Oh, What a Pity: An Ode to Paula Modersohn-Becker

1   First modern woman artist.
First woman artist to paint a self-portrait of herself naked,
while she was pregnant.

Close friend of artist Clara Westhoff and poet Rainer Maria Rilke,
you lived a short but prolific life, producing up to 80
paintings per year.

Married to a renown German landscape painter, Otto Modersohn,
you were perplexed as to what name to sign your paintings by,

and even discussed your anxiety over this decision with Rilke —
finally acceding to the hyphenated combination of your surname

and your married name, Modersohn-Becker.
Originally having met Clara Westhoff and Rainer Maria Rilke

while living in the Worpswede Artists Colony, the friendship
the three of you
enjoyed extended past your time there

perpetuated even while Clara and Rainer were in Paris
working for Rodin. You combination of naive art and your
intuitive

assimilation of impressionism was both resonant and
poignant in your painting.
Although you only sold three paintings during your life,

your work is now known worldwide. You are now
considered to have lead
the modernist movement in art, along with Pablo Picasso and
Henri Matisse.

2   A woman of her own mind, you defied your parents
    to join the Worpswede Artists Colony where you not only
        met the Rilkes

    but also Otto Modersohn, who became your husband.
    Your parents tried to intervene in your engagement, and sent
        you to cooking school,

    so she could be an attending wife. But you desperately
        "wanted to be somebody,"
    and stood firm in your following your dreams

    of becoming an accomplished painter. You frequently painted
        women
    as they gardened, as they breastfed, and as they slept.

    You died at the early age of thirty-one
    from an embolism after giving birth to your daughter,
        Mathilde. Your last words

    recorded were: *Oh, what a pity.*
    You are also known for your paintings of lemons, cherries,
        and pumpkins.

    These are mentioned in Rilke's elegy to you, his soul mate, in
        "Requiem for a Friend,"
    which is memorable for many lines, but certainly for these two:

    "For somewhere an old enmity exists
    between our life and the great works we do."

Impermanence

Shadows and light
crossing the fields this morning

over the asphalt road,
the tawny *plein* of the open,

uncut meadow,
in all of their gloss and burnish,

fill me with abundance. Although
ethereal, moving through

the *je'n sais quoi*
of slanting light and rolling hills

offers resilience through this land
of sacred geometries,

what is and is not, what is where
and then not there, in perpetual

movement, from one moment
to the next, changing

in such oscillations through
what we know as time, but

in all verity, the dewy present
is sent shimmering beyond

the sun's glare above the curve
of bent grasses, in all that ever is.

About the Author

WALLY SWIST is the author of some three dozen books and chapbooks of poetry and prose.

Among his books are *The Daodejing: A New Interpretation*, with co-authors, David Breeden and Steven Schroeder (Beaumont, TX: Lamar University Press, 2015). His book *Huang Po and the Dimensions of Love* was selected co-winner of the 2011 Crab Orchard Series Open Poetry Contest, Pulitzer Prize-winning poet Yusef Komunyakaa served as judge, and the book was published by Southern Illinois University Press in 2012. The book was nominated by Southern Illinois University Press for a National Book Award.

Swist has also published three previous books of poetry with Shanti Arts, of Brunswick, Maine: *Candling the Eggs* (2016); *The Map of Eternity* (2018); and *The Bees of the Invisible* (2019). His books of nonfiction include *Singing for Nothing: Selected Nonfiction as Literary Memoir* (Brooklyn, NY: The Operating System, 2018) and *On Beauty: Essays, Reviews, Fiction, and Plays* (New York & Lisbon: Adelaide Books, 2018).

Swist is a recipient of Artist's Fellowships in poetry from the Connecticut Commission on the Arts (1977 and 2003). He was also awarded a one-year writing residency (1998) and two back-to-back one-year writing residencies (2003–2005) at his former mentor's home, Fort Juniper, the Robert Francis Homestead, in the Cushman Village section of Amherst, Massachusetts.

Swist's work has appeared in such national periodicals such as *Commonweal*, *The North American Review*, *Rattle*, *Rolling Stone*, *Yankee Magazine*, and *Your Impossible Voice*.

He currently makes his home in western Massachusetts, where he is semi-retired and works as a freelance editor and writer.

SHANTI ARTS

NATURE ▪ ART ▪ SPIRIT

Please visit us on online
to browse our entire book catalog,
including poetry collections and fiction,
books on travel, nature, healing, art,
photography, and more.

Also take a look at our highly
regarded art and literary journal,
Still Point Arts Quarterly, which
may be downloaded for free.

www.shantiarts.com

CPSIA information can be obtained
at www.ICGtesting.com
Printed in the USA
LVHW051315280620
659166LV00001B/56